What People Are Saying

In *Decades of Gratitude, Gusto, Grit & Grace*, Minx Boren gives readers a new playbook for living big, vibrant, and fulfilling lives in the latter years of life.

—SCOTT WINTRIP, AUTHOR OF *HIGH VELOCITY HIRING: HOW TO HIRE TOP TALENT IN AN INSTANT*

Minx possesses an amazing combination of gifts which allow her to move through a lifetime observing herself and the world around her, and then to beautifully describe what she sees and feels in words that create a profound impact on the reader. In this book, she reminds each of us that life is precious and "possible" at every stage...in every moment. No one I know is filled with more Grace, Grit, Gratitude, or Gusto than Minx Boren and, having read this fabulous book, I am inspired to go out and keep growing with gusto!

—BOBETTE REEDER M.ED., MCC, PAST PRESIDENT, INTERNATIONAL COACH FEDERATION; CO-FOUNDER, THE COACH INITIATIVE; CO-FOUNDER, CONVERSATION AMONG MASTERS

This is a book not to be missed, no matter your age, no matter your sex. Minx's enlightening view of the meaning of a joyful and fulfilling life commands our consideration and attention. A terrific, provocative book.

—VALERIE RAMSEY, AUTHOR OF *CREATING WHAT'S NEXT—GRACEFULLY*; REINVENTION EXPERT; NATIONAL SPEAKERS' CIRCUIT

We "Boomers" have been thrust into a volatile, uncertain, complex and ambiguous world. Minx Boren's book *Decades of Gratitude, Gusto, Grit & Grace* is a wise woman's offering of not only how to navigate the next stage of life with grace and aliveness, but to unlock the very spirit of life's purpose anew. As a poet, leader of women, and grandmother she's plunged into life full bore, giving her the right to write an audacious book such as this.

—Patricia & Craig Neal, authors of *The Art of Convening: Authentic Engagement in Meetings, Gatherings and Conversations;* Founders, Center for Purposeful Leadership

Minx Boren has an impressive ability to integrate her personal experience, insights, and what she has picked up from continual lifelong learning into awe-inspiring poetry and prose. Most importantly she is a glorious example of what she shares in her writing. Minx has grown gracefully through the decades and this book is filled with perspectives and practical skills and habits that we can use as we age, whatever age we may be.

—Ayn Fox, Creativity and Leadership Coach

Minx Boren is a unique and amazing woman, with a voice that resonates deeply and universally. As we encounter our own life cycles we determine what and who we are at any given moment. Minx helps us expand our exploration through her soul-touching poetry and her heart-touching personal experiences. Doors and windows of potential and possibility open for us all. If you are seeking your own *gratitude, gusto, grit, and grace* as you grow in years and decades, I couldn't imagine a better guiding light than this book!

—Bobbi Gemma, MCC, author of *Thought Bites, Wisdoms and Other Funky Stuff;* President, The Gemma Group

The poetry and writings of Minx Boren provide a wise, reflective insight into the depths of the human spirit.

—PAUL STRICKLAND, RETIRED HUMAN RESOURCES EXECUTIVE

Minx pens poems that often make me cry and laugh in a single reading. She cuts straight to that universal heart of the matter, which is so often forgotten in divisive times.

—VONDA VADEN BATES, CEO, 10TH DOT®

Some authors teach. Some inspire. Some reveal the inner depths of what we hold sacred and pure. Some give voice to the unspeakable within us and around us. Minx Boren's writing includes all of this and much more. Experiencing her work is to mark the terrain of our life, coming back to this new ground again and again for nourishment. This is the book we keep under our pillow and pray it insumes each of our restful and waking moments.

—EDDIE MARMOL, EXECUTIVE COACH

Decades of Gratitude, Gusto, Grit & Grace is compelling reading. Minx Boren doesn't hold back—she regales you with real-life stories—of crisis, of wonder, of learning, of daring. Boren marshals her formidable life experience into themes, each chapter exploring a quality, a strength she grew into and now invites you to do the same. She charms you with her voice, her way of making you feel that you too could easily slip into a fuller humanity with just a tweak here, a shift there. Her perspective as a longtime life coach serves to add to the depth of her observations and offerings.

I think others will especially relate to her journey from shy introvert to powerful teacher, coach and advocate. I know I did.

—EVAN GRIFFITH, AUTHOR OF *BURN, BABY, BURN: SPARK THE CREATIVE SPIRIT WITHIN*; ADVOCATE FOR ALL THINGS CREATIVE AT NOTESFORCREATORS.COM

OTHER BOOKS BY MINX BOREN

Poetry Collections

Soul Notes

Soul Notes Too

Ripe: A Collection of Passionate Poetry and Pears
in collaboration with artist Patti Burris

Feeling My Way: 99 Poetic Journeys

Blue Mountain Arts Publications

Healing Is a Journey:
Find Your Own Path to Hope, Recovery, and Wellness

Friendship Is a Journey:
A Celebration of True Connection and Deep Caring

Authentic Woman Enterprises LLC Publications
in collaboration with Rev. Marsha Lehman PCC

Hold Me—A More than Coloring Book

My BLIP Journal: because wisdom doesn't have to be wordy

MenoPAUSE for Pleasure

PJ Party Retreat Book—Women Really Love to Have Fun

Getting in Touch with Your InnerCoach™ about Love
Audio program and guidebook

The Authentic Woman Coaching Collaborative
with Rev. Marsha Lehman PCC and Deborah Roth MA, PCC

The Authentic Woman Play Book:
Daily Discoverings of Your Divine Feminine—Winter

The Authentic Woman Play Book:
Daily Discoverings of Your Divine Feminine—Spring

The Authentic Woman Play Book:
Daily Discoverings of Your Divine Feminine—Summer

The Authentic Woman Play Book:
Daily Discoverings of Your Divine Feminine—Fall

PATH Consulting
in collaboration with Cynthia Gracey, Esq.

Visionheart: A Journey to Values and Purpose

Decades

of
Gratitude, Gusto,
Grit & Grace

MINX BOREN, MCC

Dear Mary Elaine
With gratitude
for the gift of your full
presence.
Happy 70th
Minx

Decades of Gratitude, Gusto, Grit & Grace

Published by
Coach Minx Inc.
www.CoachMinx.com

ISBN: 978-0-9702550-3-7

Cover and interior design:
Gary A. Rosenberg • www.thebookcouple.com

Author photo:
Lynn Hernandez Studios

Printed in the United States of America

Contents

To all the gracious and gutsy ones—
those I know, those I know about,
and those I may never know or know about—
who choose again and again
to embrace life at every age and stage—

It matters.

You matter.

Thank you.

I so enjoy good and feisty words
the kind that convey far and away
more than a dictionary
definition can possibly capture.

I am thinking about *gutsy*
rolling the letters around on my tongue
letting its guttural sound
vibrate around in my throat.

If only I could swallow it whole
and embody that quality
of clear and courageous presence
by simply willing it into being...my being.

But it takes *grit* and *gumption*
a clarity of conviction and
the will and willingness to step up
ever so boldly and embody my Truth.

No matter the gusty winds
that howl relentlessly at my most
strongly held beliefs and my most
deeply felt hunches and inklings

gutsiness is about holding fast
to values, standing up
to the vicissitudes of life and
facing the prickly fickleness of fortune.

And so I must make time
to step out beyond the ongoing
onslaught of conflicting ideas
and everyone else's good intentions

in order to seek my own plucky way
through the forest of advice
and flurry of information that threaten
to obscure my very own path.

And all this must be done with *grace*
and true graciousness
with the sincerity of my own *gratitude*
and the ongoing opening of my own heart.

Growing through the Years
with Gratitude, Gusto, Grit & Grace

An Invitation

find your way
it doesn't have to be
the only way
or the right way
it just needs to be
real... really
inspired by your gut
and fueled by your
grit and embellished
by your gusto

There is an adage that goes, "We teach what we want to learn." In the course of authoring this book, I have come to learn that, for me, the same holds true for writing. During the more than two years that it took for the manuscript to take shape and find its way onto the page, things have changed and, more importantly, I have changed. Looking at my life through the lens of the 4 Gs—gratitude, gusto, grit, and grace—I have been able to recognize and celebrate the ways I have stepped into my own as well as admit to the ways I have fallen short. This self-confrontational soul searching has led to the need to actually grow boldly and attentively through the process and courageously step up to face challenges in my own life. My hope and intention is that the same will hold true for you.

Within these pages is an invitation for you to consider your life from the multiple perspectives of past, present and future. In this way, you are encouraged to first acknowledge: how you have navigated your years to this point in time, what you have done with your precious life thus far, how you have survived and thrived along the way, who you are now, and what might be showing up on the horizon beckoning you onward.

This book is about growing ongoingly year by year and decade by decade. It recognizes our capacity to continue to structure our lives in significant and fulfilling ways as we journey through our days. It acknowledges our yearning to develop into our most authentic and passionate selves. Each chapter offers an opportunity to cultivate an understanding of the ways that stepping into our middle and later years can be a special and spectacular opportunity to both reflect upon and acknowledge how we have made our way so far, what we have taken on, what we have overcome, what we have accomplished, and what we have chosen to walk toward and away from. It offers a vantage point from which to see the fullness of our lives as well as where we might want to go from here.

Let me be clear. This quest is not necessarily about choosing to do or take on one more thing. Some of us feel as though we have reached a point when we are drawn toward intentionally walking away from many of the demands placed upon us, recognizing all that we have already taken on, and moving beyond all that we have already accomplished in order to simply be...at ease and relaxed, relishing a sense of quiet satisfaction, and seeking to devote time to being with those we love. We are in a time of revisiting and reflecting on life in general and our life in particular. Or perhaps, at last the moment has arrived to simply enjoy ourselves...to laugh and play more, to travel without having to adhere to a tight schedule or time constraints, to explore new hobbies for the joy of it without any measurable milestones to achieve, or to sit quietly and simply enjoy a good read. And there are those of us who are looking for new mountains to climb and new challenges to take on, who don't want to feel stifled or held back because of our age. There is no one right way to grow into our later decades.

Growing (b)older is no small task. Both personally and in the larger scheme of things, these times call for nothing less than our most audacious, intrepid, and committed effort to shape these years into something worthy of the gift of our time here on earth. How can we step vibrantly into the roles we may now choose to take on and how can we positively turn away from that which no longer serves us? How do we, with commitment and enthusiasm, embrace the activities in which we opt to engage? How do we give ourselves permission to let go of the list of "coulda shoulda" stuff that no longer calls to us?

For me, it all starts with gratitude and it seems to also require gusto and gumption, grit and grace, good will and graciousness, goodness and a great attitude, generosity and genuineness, *and* a whole lot more. Finding our way through these very grown-up years seems to ask of us nothing less than our total dedication to take excellent care of ourselves and to thrive, while also contributing to a world that works for everyone...but with discernment so that our choices also work for us. It requires all these "G" qualities to let go of previous habits and identities that no longer resonate in order to find the ones that are appropriate and authentic *now*. It's about finding our *now* rhythm and style. It's about doing more if we so choose, and it's about also giving ourselves permission to do less if that is what works...or, perhaps, some apt new mix of both. It's the Goldilocks solution—not too hot, not too cold, but rather just the right pace of grace for this time in our lives.

The Gift of a Question

I have been a life coach by profession for more than twenty years. Coaching is above all a process of inquiry designed to inspire your inklings, deep knowings, and wisdom. My training has taught me to love good questions...challenging and provocative inquiries that get juices flowing and invite all sorts of *awarenesses* to bubble up. The central questions at the heart of growing ongoingly are, *"What matters to you now?" "What is the big question you are facing in your own life right now and how are you choosing to address it?" "Who are you beyond your roles and jobs and all that you do and have done and in what ways does this identity satisfy and serve you now?" "And what else?" "What are the questions you are yearning to explore?"*

This book is filled with my stories and the stories of others with whom I have had the privilege to spend deep soul-searching time. It is about the questions that arise from these stories (many of which are italicized within each chapter so they are easy for you to find *and,* hopefully, pause to consider). And, it's about the methods and tools that evolved from dealing with the happenings in these stories, strategies that can support you along the way to *what now* and *what next* because ultimately this book is for and about you. It's about offering you, the reader, the gift of stimulating questions and interesting queries and then inviting you to listen deeply and mindfully to the understandings that arise from within. It's about calling upon you to consider all the *AHAs!* and pivotal moments in your life that have shaped you and guided your choices. It's about paying attention and articulating what matters and what counts for you. And it's about pausing long enough to admire the view from whatever decade of life you are now privileged to be experiencing. What might be awakened and revealed within you in the process of making your way through these pages? What might shift and transform within you through this very private investigation?

So, here's the thing that is particularly important for both me as the writer and for you as the reader. Books have always been my friends and my teachers. My hope and intention is that this one will become one of yours. This book is not meant to be prescriptive. I do not have your answers. Only you do. So the grand purpose of this book is to inspire you to search for and articulate your own perceptions—the ideas and inklings that have shaped and reshaped your life to this point in time, the values and virtues that you live by, the starry ideals and significant understandings by which you navigate your days and, in so doing, find both fulfillment and joy.

The Gift of Encouragement

Each question, inquiry, and prompt in the book is meant to encourage you to examine your thoughts and feelings. To reap the full value of what you are reading, I invite you—actually I urge you—to participate fully, question by question, so as to discover your Self through these pages. You might choose to capture your reflections in your own private journal or you might use the ideas presented as prompts for a discussion group. Note that scribbling in the margins of this book is also a marvelous opportunity to make it your own. I have scribbled in the margins and underlined and earmarked pages and added sticky notes in hundreds of books. I like picturing you doing the same with this one. No need for elaborate or well-constructed essays…just words and random ideas, inklings, and alternative views duly noted and expanded upon to whatever degree suits your time and temperament.

The Gift of Self-Discovery

Above all, enjoy the journey. At some point in our lives, we owe it to ourselves to be curious about who in the world we are, to take inventory of how and why we, both intentionally and inadvertently, plot a course for our lives through our choices and actions, and to pay attention to the ways we learn to steer by our own True North. This is one of the significant opportunities of the passage through the decades.

With all great wishes for your fulfilling future,

Coach Minx

Why this book? Why me? Why now?

Many years ago, while participating in a sweat lodge ceremony, I had a profound experience of being in touch with my lineage, my bloodline, as well as the countless women who have walked this earth before me. I share more about this particularly life-changing event in the section titled *AHA! Moments*. What is important to note here is that it was during that startling incident that I was given a glimpse of how I am the repository of thousands of years of history, experience, knowledge, and wisdom, *and* it was now my responsibility—my work in the world—to use all this to inspire women to honor the shoulders upon which they now stand and to step into their own power in order to significantly express their own gifts and talents.

If we are fortunate, there comes a time when we reach a portentous threshold—a vantage point from where we can look backwards and forward to see the vastness and the intricacies of our journeys, both individually and as part of something much greater than our individual selves. For me, turning seventy and beyond has become that threshold.

I am someone who has written books—lots of books. Actually, I have been writing for most of my life—starting with private journals and poetry and then expanding more publicly to essays, articles, and more. At this moment in time I am called to dive even deeper and write more intimately about my own journey as well as the experiences, stories, and wise words that have been shared with me over many years. I do this not because I have it all figured out. Not by a long shot. Rather it is because, as a coach, I have learned the value of asking great questions and then staying curious and nonjudgmental as to what shows up on the page, in spoken communications, in my life, and in the lives of my friends and clients.

I have been a life coach for almost twenty years. I love my profession. Coaching is a process of inquiry and this book is, above all, an invitation to inquire deeply into your own ideas and inklings. Having kept a journal for more than sixty years, I have learned the satisfaction that comes from allowing oneself time to reflect and mull and ponder *ongoingly*. I am continually surprised by what shows up on the page when I write with neither agenda nor outline...simply as an opportunity to contemplate anything/everything, receptive to the insights that show up as a reward for the time spent.

Beyond coming from the perspective of coaching, I also write from the vantage point of all that I have been privileged to learn as a motivational speaker, a writer and poet, a facilitator of group conversations, *and* a human being. What I really want to do on these pages is create an inspirational manifesto *(platform, philosophy, declaration, statement, proposal, strategy—call it what you will)* for these later years not only for myself and my cronies, colleagues, and clients but also for those coming up the path behind us.

In her book *Big Magic,* Elizabeth Gilbert talks about the creative flow within us waiting to bubble up and burst forth in magical ways. Although she had been writing for many years, Ms. Gilbert also speaks about how she couldn't elucidate her personal manifesto on creativity until she had lived the principles long enough and successfully published enough to trust that they work...at least for her. That's exactly how I feel about growing through the decades with gratitude, gusto, grit, and grace. It's not easy to age in a powerful and productive way. Dare I even use the word *age* considering *age-ism*—the current bias/prejudice against getting old? It's an act of courage and conviction. What I am discovering is that it requires attention, intention, willpower, determination, ongoing self-reflection and soul-searching...as well as enthusiasm and a certain lightness of being to make it all worthwhile.

This is the book I have felt called to write for a while. Now I am inviting you, dear reader and seeker, to join me in this exploration of what it means to be fully human and to live a fulfilling life.

A Guide to How
This Book Is Organized

As I began to gather ideas, I realized that they fell into two main categories, beginning with a personal collection of *AHA! Moments* ...times when my perception or worldview has shifted, and some new awareness or possibility has taken shape. These revealing change points are unique to me *and* we all have them. They can arise because of words in a book or words spoken. They might flash onto center screen because of a particularly serendipitous meeting or occurrence, an extraordinary (or even rather ordinary) experience or something/anything that was particularly provocative. And, of course, many of these *AHAs!* do grow out of universal yet individualized milestones such as entering a new decade or phase of life. Because they span a lifetime of discoveries, I have divided these *AHA! Moments* into two parts: *Boldness Matters* and *Growing Ongoingly.*

It cannot be denied that being seventy and beyond offers a perspective worthy of consideration. The last part of this book is devoted to some of the observations rendered more clearly visible from the vantage point of the **Decades of Gratitude, Gusto, Grit & Grace**—the ways growing older both shapes and softens us, the ways our values change and the ways they stay the same, and the ways we come to understand that *today is a good day* and that *today is always a beginning.*

This book is more a collection of compositions than of chapters, each one related to the whole and each one a singular idea. Together they are meant to create a flow of substantive thoughts that are more than the sum of their individual content. While I may be the author of these particular reflections, all were composed around scintillating sparks gathered from the ideas and inspirations of countless others, many of whom I talk about and quote. I tell you this up front because a particularly important premise of mine is that none of us is wise enough alone.

As you begin, my grand intention is that you find your own wisdom sparked all along your journey through these pages. My grand hope is that, at the end, you too will have arrived at some new level of understanding and inspiration from where to begin again...because each ending is also a beginning.

AHA! Moments—
An Introduction

We've all experienced them—those startling and often unexpected moments that change our thinking, our beliefs, our lives. Sometimes it's about a lightbulb going off in our mind's eye so that we can see something clearly, perhaps for the first time. Other times, it's a gut feeling that something is absolutely right...or wrong. Or it might be an experience that takes our breath away and allows our heart to reach a new level of understanding or compassion or courage. It might also arise as a newly visceral understanding of something we have heard a thousand times—"Just wait until you have kids," or "It's not over till it's over," or "Good things come to those who wait," or "You are what you think," or "Don't try. Just do." Suddenly you recognize the veracity and wisdom of what you once ignored or discounted as mere platitude. No matter how an *AHA!* shows up, once its true meaning captivates us, we can never think about that particular idea or person or situation or experience in exactly the same way we did before.

I remember a woman who participated in a group experience I facilitated. Every time she spoke she explained away what was wrong with her life and the reasons why she was stuck on her mother's lack of love and attention. Finally, I asked if she too has been a terrible mother, after having had such a poor role model. She was startled by my question and declared that it was quite the opposite. She is a terrific mother who has a wonderful relationship with her daughter. "Why might that be?" I asked. "Because I never want to be anything like my mother and I do everything quite differently," she answered. I then asked if, perhaps, there was a hidden gift in her difficult childhood. And then came her

AHA! moment as she understood all the ways in which she had positively shaped her life and expanded her capacity to be caring so as to counteract that negativity. With her new awareness, I challenged her to make a choice to not tell her story in such a discouraging way again nor to use those childhood stories as an excuse for not pursuing what she wanted in life. Instead, I invited her to find ways to speak about the impact of her life lessons and to use the energy of those emotions to make new choices. About a year later, I bumped into her, and she thanked me for the gift of both that question and challenge. During a long conversation, she told me how she had stopped rambling on about all that past stuff. No longer does she use the difficulties of those early years as an excuse. It was delightful to hear about how her whole life has become easier and happier because of it.

I love to ask people about their favorite or most poignant *AHA! moments*. Because the question elicits such varied responses, I have taken to writing them down. I will share just a few of them here so that you can glean the richness and transformational possibilities embedded in these sudden new ways of thinking and feeling about things.

BARBARA—*AHA! I can (learn to) do that.*

Barbara's mother was a Holocaust survivor. When Barbara came to the United States with her mother as a young girl they were very poor, and she needed to find work but had no formal training. Barbara learned that to land a job (and forge ahead) she first needed to say, "Yes I can do that," and then figure out how.

BILL—*AHA! It is I who must speak up for myself.*

Bill had an *AHA! moment* that involved the realization that if he didn't speak up for himself, toot his own horn, and let others know about his accomplishments, he would never advance up the ladder or be as successful as he could be. In the busy world of big business, he recognized that he could not expect people to simply notice his intelligence and competence if he wasn't willing to be his own best spokesperson.

CHARLENE—*AHA! I can be and do anything I choose.*
After taking the school's IQ test at the age of ten, the principal called Charlene into her office and said emphatically, "You really can be ANYTHING you want to be." Charlene believed her words and went on to have a very satisfying career in business, which included mastering computer technology back in the days when there were very few women in the field.

DRAZIA—*AHA! Just because I can doesn't mean I should!*
Drazia offered the following examples: lifting heavy or bulky things is possible but not usually smart. Neither is climbing up on a ladder.
AHA! Saying "no" is an option.
This realization has made her more discerning about her old habit of saying "YES" too quickly when asked to do something for others. Just because she is capable of the task doesn't mean she should take it on. It's essential to first consider the impact on time and/or resources. A person can say "NO" and the world won't end.
Two others worth mentioning are:
AHA! I don't always have to know all the steps in order to begin.
AHA! Don't believe everything you think.

IONE—*AHA! Other people have worldviews and beliefs that differ from my own.*
In preparation for a vacation in Japan, Ione decided to read several books on Eastern culture and thought. She realized, for the first time in her "sheltered" life, that other people think differently and have dramatically different world views from her own. This was the beginning of a growing curiosity to know more as well as acquiring a more expansive way of seeing things.

JENIFER—*AHA! With freedom comes responsibility.*
When Jenifer was seven years old she was asked to write an essay about freedom for school. She asked her dad to help her understand what

that meant. He explained that, with the gift of freedom and the ability to make choices about your own life, come the responsibility to make good choices that impact you and those around you in positive ways.

JOY—*AHA! I can reinvent myself using old skills in new ways.*
Joy's first career was as a music teacher. As she was becoming restless and wanting to do more, at some point she had the clear realization that she could bring that talent into a new career as a counselor. That intention propelled her into action to do whatever was necessary to earn a degree in counseling and to build her professional practice.

MEL—*AHA! I have always tried to live my life as a gentleman.*
Ever since Mel can remember, his father, by example, instilled in him the importance of always being a gentleman. His dad was a shining example of being courteous and attentive to all those around him, never losing his temper or speaking inappropriately. The *AHA!* came years later when Mel realized that, throughout his life, he has tried to emulate his father and live up to this way of being.

Sometimes these *AHA! moments* appear out of the blue—unexpected and unbidden—with a definite and immediate jolt to our awareness. Many times, though, as I have asked the question, it took a while for the answers to arise because, as Drazia noted, "Many of the big *AHAS!* from my earlier days have become the water I swim in, so it is difficult to identify them all these years later." In these cases, it is only when we take the time to focus on the past that we can, in retrospect, see the impact of something as simple and taken for granted as a father whose demeanor was always calm and polite. The "lesson" might come to light the first time we are triggered and are at the crossroads of either reacting belligerently or responding with poise and presence. Something within us recalls the lesson of a key figure or mentor in our life and we make an inspired choice for ourselves, recognizing how that particular way of being or doing was instilled in us early on.

I so love serendipities. Just as I was putting the finishing touches on this chapter I received a note from a dear friend (in response to a poem I wrote) that is so germane to this conversation I am including it here.

LABLE—"Now that I have the time to participate in many discussions and discussion-groups, the question I get asked most often is, 'How can we know what is spiritual and what is not?' So, I have looked deeply into that question, and here is the answer I give now, 'Whatever makes me feel more connected is of the Spirit. Whatever makes me feel more separate is of the Ego.' When I tell this to people, their faces light up with an *AHA! moment*. They *grasp* it, and they can use it to discern the spiritual from the egotistical in their own lives. What is so powerful about that yardstick is that it offers no prescription or proscription. What makes one person feel connected may make another person feel separate. It is up to each person to map their spiritual quests by their own feelings."

Before you turn the page, it might be worth your while to grab a piece of paper and jot down your own AHA! moments while they are fresh in your mind. Then, as you read through those I have written about, you might also start to recall when a similar (or quite opposite) *AHA!* arose in your own consciousness.

PART ONE

AHA! MOMENTS— BOLDNESS MATTERS

"It takes courage to grow up and become who we really are."

~EE CUMMINGS, AMERICAN POET

It Takes Gratitude, Gusto, Grit & Grace

"Be kind, for everyone you meet is carrying a hard burden."
~Ian MacLaren, pseudonym for Rev. John Watson—
Scotsman, author

. . . **a**nd, at some time or another, that includes you and me. Sometimes it requires all our time and focus to get to a place of feeling safe and healthy, clothed and fed. But sometimes being safe and healthy, clothed and fed, as well as being blessed with a fair amount of creature comforts, still doesn't seem like "enough." Thriving into our later years and cultivating an ongoing sense of fulfillment takes a lot.

While thinking about the essence of this book I was struck with an *AHA!* realization about the importance of these four "Gs." It all starts with gratitude…every day…for the gift of that day, for the beauty all around us, for the capacity to care and to love, for the opportunities to live satisfying lives no matter our circumstances, for whatever our body and mind are still capable of as well as for those who offer us a helping hand when we can no longer manage things on our own in these changing and vulnerable bodily vessels that contain our spirit and our soul.

And yes, it absolutely takes gusto…a certain determined zest for life and the inner capacity to stoke the fires of passion in one's heart again and again. What one person sees as a formidable obstacle another approaches as a momentous mountain to climb and musters up the courage and commitment to just do it. What one person experiences as the frustration of no longer being at the center of attention or the action

another embraces as a clear choice to slow down and smell the proverbial flowers and to just as passionately enjoy life at a more leisurely pace.

Which is why it also takes grit...lots of it. Every opportunity and
every challenge invite us to find the will and willingness to meet them
with all we've got—our strengths and talents, our lifetime of experience and knowledge, the core values and virtues that sustain us, and,
of course, all the compassion and love of which we are capable. On the
other hand, I know of many wise men and women in their fifth, sixth,
or seventh decades who find that it takes equal conviction to step away
from the busy mainstreams of life in order to create a certain spaciousness for reflection, self-caring, and even "indulgent" frivolity. Sometimes their decision to not engage in doing and accomplishing more
and more is looked at critically rather than with respect and curiosity.

Beyond that it takes endless grace. It's about grace in the sense of
showing up with poise and dignity, even in the face of difficulty or crisis.
It's about grace in the sense of kindness and decency. It's about grace in
the sense of open-hearted and open-minded availability. It is also about
the divine grace that guides and enfolds us every step of the way.

Then, beyond all this, it still takes a whole lot more—courage and
commitment, integrity and intelligence, endurance and enthusiasm,
good will and a good attitude, generosity and genuineness, a sense of
humor and a sense of the value of playfulness. There are stories everywhere of people finding the wherewithal to pull themselves up by the
bootstraps and out beyond whatever life has thrown their way—sometimes by just staying afloat, sometimes by finding a way to do more (or
less) and, mostly, by not succumbing to dismay.

As I was writing this chapter, I was shocked to hear that a friend
of mine had been pushed over from behind at an airport and had lost
several of her front teeth when she fell. Two emergency surgeries later,
she is just beginning the long process of putting her body and her life
back together. Yet, knowing her, somehow she will find a way without abandoning the legal practice she so enjoys. Another friend with
advanced neuropathy has had to resort to using a walker, and yet she is

still out in the world teaching coaching skills in colleges and corpora-
tions. A third friend is doing her darnedest, while coping with debilitating spinal pain, to continue to volunteer with ex-convicts, teaching
alternatives to violence. Ram Dass, author of *Be Here Now,* is a spiritual
leader who first inspired me decades ago when I heard him speak at a
conference. He suffered a stroke awhile back and yet has found ways to
continue to live with meaning and purpose, declaring that *this* [physical
challenge] IS his work in the world now. I can only pray for even a frac-
tion of that kind of strength and courage should it ever come to that. I
cannot know what I may or may not be capable of. None of us can. But
we can continue to do our best to hone our grit and gratitude and build
our resilience muscle in order to make the most of our precious and
unpredictable life.

On the opposite end of the continuum of life choices, I want to tell
you about two highly accomplished people I know who have enjoyed
significant and meaningful careers. One has retired to North Carolina
and delights in no longer having to set an alarm clock, preferring to
allow his own internal rhythm lead the way into each day. The other,
in her mid-seventies and recently married, has chosen to use more of
her time simply enjoying her role as part of a couple and the unhurried
hours that are available to her now. Having spent her life driven by the
many well-meaning messages of others encouraging her to be active,
proactive, and achieve more and more, this new commitment requires
that she move beyond long-held beliefs and habits in order to be at
peace with her new more leisurely and self-nurturing choices. Life is
calling to each of them in newly appealing ways.

Then there is the middle ground of those looking to slow down yet
continue to share their gifts, talents, and expertise in more limited ways.
One woman, a longtime hospice nurse who was actually instrumental
in raising the funds for a new hospice home in Connecticut, has now
chosen to be a part-time volunteer consultant in Palm Beach County
for a non-profit that is looking to create a local hospice home. Here
in my community, there are a number of residents who volunteer at a

local grade school enrichment program, offering yoga classes, meditation classes, and classes on all sorts of topics running the gamut from minding their manners to managing money.

There is no one way, no right way, to navigate these middle years and beyond, only the ways that feel most satisfying to each of us.

An Ethical Perspective

"Ethics: moral principles that govern a person's behavior or the conducting of an activity."
~OXFORD ENGLISH DICTIONARY

"Ethics is a set of values that consistently guides our behaviors."
~MARKKULA CENTER FOR APPLIED ETHICS

Curiosity about this journey called *Life* and my place in the vast scheme of things has always been a driving force in my own life. It's such a miracle and a puzzlement that we even exist at all. When I was very young I remember lying in bed every night and asking myself over and over and over, "Who am I?" I would answer with my name and where I lived and where I went to school. The voice would say, "Yes BUT who am I?" I would answer, "a daughter, a student, a friend, an American, a...*whatever.*" Then the voice would say, "Yes, but WHO AM I?" And so it would go, on and on, until my small body would seem to merge with those I loved, those I didn't know, all planetary beings, and finally the earth and the stars and the great beyond. Only then would I fall asleep.

Along with my sense of wonderment, I somehow also developed a sense of responsibility. If I belonged to all this, what was I supposed to do about it? What did it mean to truly belong? And how was I supposed to behave so as to actively participate in belonging?

Given my intense curiosity, I was very fortunate because, from grades three through eight, I attended the Ethical Culture School in Brooklyn, New York. It was an enchanting place and was even housed in a fairytale type of stone castle. The school offered, as part of its mandatory curriculum, ethics classes emphasizing the common themes of all religions, the universal values that all men and women recognize, and what it means to live an ethical life. Later, in college and graduate school, I studied French literature (which really meant the philosophies expressed in the various literary works), and so I was able to take another deep dive into the underpinnings of what it means to be fully human.

Over the years there have been many *AHA! moments* on my search for meaning. Actually, it was Viktor Frankl's book *Man's Search for Meaning* that provided a particularly strong jolt of awakening early on. Some members of my family were killed in the Holocaust and I grew up with the stories of those people, those times, and the war (several of my uncles served in WWII). I thought a lot about *how is one to live in the face of such hatred and cruelty?* Dr. Frankl, an Austrian neurologist and psychiatrist, as well as a Holocaust survivor, had experienced the worst of the worst in those camps. Yet, he found his answer to the question of how to live through his conviction that life always has meaning. No matter the shock of inmates first arriving at the camp and their reactions of depersonalization, bitterness, and disillusionment which often led to apathy, Frankl saw that the meaning of life can be found in every moment of living. He determined that life continues to have meaning, even in suffering and death. Interestingly, the German title of his book literally translates to: *Nevertheless Say 'Yes' to Life: A Psychologist Experiences the Concentration Camps.* Frankl concluded that a prisoner's psychological reactions are not solely the result of the imposed conditions of his life, but also from the freedom of choice he always has as to his response—be it kindness, compassion, courage, determination, service to others, or the whole gamut of positive and ethical human behavior. Above all, the inner hold a prisoner has on his spiritual self and sanity ultimately rested on having hope in the future—not only for himself but also for humanity. In the end, Frankl believed it is essential that we serve others, our ancestors, and God, all of whom would expect to not be disappointed.

Hope and kindness, compassion and courage, ethical behavior in the face of even the worst of tragedies—these were guiding principles that inspired me. If Frankl could find these qualities within himself and observe them in others, if he could keep hope alive, then perhaps so could I. My father's cousin Izzy was a young boy when he was sent into the camps. He survived because he was clever, resourceful, and lucky. The story I remember best was how each day Izzy had to make a choice about the stale, moldy piece of bread that was his ration. He could eat it all at once to momentarily assuage his hunger, he could keep it in his pocket and break off tiny pieces to soothe him during the day or he could give it to someone else who was in greater need. That a young boy could understand this was astonishing to me. *Could I have done that?* I don't know.

What I do know is that another pivotal *AHA!* showed up when I first read the words of the Dalai Lama, "My religion is kindness." Having spent my childhood studying, being inspired by, *and* questioning various religious philosophies, this statement positively worked for me as a clear guiding principle by which to navigate. This explanation was enough for me to hang my hat on and stop the need to construct more complex explanations of what in the world I believe and believe in.

According to research in the field of positive psychology, an essential aspect of building personal awareness and making wise choices has to do with clearly knowing one's highest values and navigating through life using them as a guiding star. A group of psychologists developed the Values in Action (VIA) Survey of Character Strengths—a free online assessment. It is a twenty-minute questionnaire that results in a rather accurate individual "ranking" of twenty-four character strengths.

What is especially remarkable about these twenty-four strengths is that they are classified under six core moral virtues: Wisdom and Knowledge, Courage, Humanity, Justice, Temperance, and Transcendence, "that emerge consensually across culture and throughout time." This descriptive is from *Character Strengths and Virtues: A Handbook and Classification* by Christopher Peterson and Martin Seligman. I cannot begin to do justice or even summarize the eight-hundred-page volume and all that went into determining and developing these classifications and strengths. What I will say is that they are at the heart of what it means to be human. And they are definitely worth delving into in pursuit of leading a significant and satisfying life. If you are interested, an easy place to start is by looking at your strengths and what you value most. Go to: https://www.authentichappiness.sas.upenn.edu/testcenter and take the VIA Survey of Character Strengths. You will receive a list of your top five strengths. Be sure to also access your full list of twenty-four strengths assembled in order of preference according to your responses. Here's another thought: you might want to ask a friend or two to do the same. Then share stories about your highest strengths and how you have used/are using them as a compass to make choices.

Finally, and most recently, I had the opportunity to attend the Ethics Connections Program, a three-part seminar given by the Center for Applied Ethics at Palm Beach State College. This series is part of a broad initiative "to build and sustain a culture of ethics in Palm Beach County." Brilliantly conceived and constructed, the program was initiated based on the premise that we cannot change that about which we are not aware. Part One of the program offers an overview of what ethical excellence means and provides tools, skills, and strategies to address emerging ethical challenges along with an action plan for sustained ethical readiness. Part Two provides an assessment, called the *Ethical Lens Inventory*™ so that each participant understands the values that influence their own ethical reasoning and choices and those of others. Part Three—Giving Voice to Values—presents practical approaches to recognize, clarify, speak, and effectively act on one's values when conflicts arise.

Revisiting Viktor Frankl's emphasis on the importance of finding meaning in life in general and in our lives in particular, this program gives me hope in troubled times that there are intelligent, thoughtful, and powerful ways we can approach and confront the issues of our day.

Discovering Myself on the Page

words tumbling from otherwhere
pen gliding across icy white terrain
disturbing the pristine surface
leaving behind a trail of thoughts
*rushing up from my soul**

Journal writing is a process of self-reflection that can reap ongoing rewards. I've been keeping a journal, actually lots of them, since I was a young girl. The early years of my entries resembled typical "dear diary" recollections of day by day occurrences. Over time, writing in my diary became not only a place to record events but also an opportunity to learn about myself. Through the years I have explored many varied ways and styles of journal keeping, ranging from Ira Progoff's dialogue process to *List Yourself* exercises popularized by Ilene Segalove and Paul Bob Velick, from travel journals (because being away allows for great opportunities for both self-discovery and quiet contemplation) to revealing mind-maps drawn free-handedly onto large sheets of paper, from using quotes and poetry as "prompts" for diving deeply into my own responsive thoughts to autobiographical writing and stream of consciousness techniques—a method made famous by Julia Cameron in *The Artist's Way*.

The overarching *AHA!* from these various experiments with writing, scribbling, and doodling is that all these methodologies allow me to shape vague thoughts and feelings into concrete and coherent language.

---

* Minx Boren, *Soul Notes,* (Palm Beach Gardens, FL: Fourfold Path Inc., 2000): Page 52.

It is a way to understand and prioritize the incessant chattering of the mind in personally meaningful and useful ways. Reflective writing is a way to create one's own unique map for journeying through life with clarity and purpose as well as being a powerful tool for self-discovery. It serves as a worthwhile practice for making the inner voices of one's heart, mind, spirit, and soul more audible. It's a tricky business—this willingness to know thyself more deeply. Putting words on paper takes that risk to the next level, demanding that we more clearly shape our thoughts into cohesive language. The pages of one's journal are an invitation to disclose and declare what is so for us in the moment. When journaling, I often feel vulnerable and completely exposed—like lying naked on the page. At the same time, my writings and ramblings become a poignant affirmation of my truest Self.

Ultimately the effectiveness of journaling as an inner navigational instrument depends above all upon three things:

1. the willingness to be completely honest with oneself

2. the commitment to regularly set aside time for the contemplative practice to blossom

3. the decision to let go of unreasonable standards and expectations concerning both one's ability to write and the worthiness or validity of what one has to say

One reason why journal-keeping can be so effective is that it becomes a tool for creating some inner spaciousness. We cannot fill what is already full. There can be no room for change and growth unless we are willing to examine and let go of our limiting thoughts and those deeply held viewpoints that no longer serve us. To journal is to empty ourselves, to bring into the light of day our most tenaciously held convictions and assumptions, joys and heartaches, hopes and fears—for the purpose of careful examination and release. There is a certain discernment that blossoms in the process of being willing to scrutinize long-held opinions and short-sighted views. What I have noticed over the years is that many of my perspectives, my likes and dislikes, my desires and disillusionments, are transitory. So are my moods, which can shift and shimmy moment to moment. Through this process of journaling I have also come to understand that rarely am I as *stuck* as I believe myself to be while attempting to capture it all on paper. Life is about fluidity and flow, something about which I become more aware as I discover myself on the page week by week and year after year. There is a freedom in this discernment that serves me well.

We all learn, create, and relate to our world in different ways. Some of us are organized, others not so much. Some of us are verbal, others are more visual or experiential. Not everyone will approach journaling the same way. It is important for each of us to find our own style and method. All that is needed is a commitment to the practice and a surrender to the momentum of discovering oneself on the page, however it unfolds and evolves.

Here is one important caveat about journal writing in general— never leave your journal on a negative note. This is a lesson I learned the hard way. I have ranted and raged and released all sorts of profanities and negativities onto the pages of my journal, allowing the act of writing to serve as an emotional "mind dump" and catharsis. Then there was this *AHA! moment* when I realized that if, at the end of all my wretched ramblings, I simply walked away drained and disheartened, then I would miss the gift and the possibilities available because of all the difficult inner dredging I had worked through. I also recognized that I actually gave too much "power" to all those nasty notions I had disclosed by not at least beginning to confront them. By going the extra mile and staying the course until I could find at least one positive step or shift, I could start to turn things around. This enabled me to transform the writings into a great gift—an opportunity to move toward a more positive and meaningful approach to achieving what I wanted for myself.

Here is one more suggestion about another popular type of journaling that has served me well. The art of letter writing has deep roots.

In centuries past much communication transpired through penned correspondence. Nowadays brief emails and Tweets seem to suffice. But I am old-fashioned enough to still enjoy writing letters and *thank you* notes by hand. For more than thirty-five years, since my mother died, I have been writing her a letter every Christmas Day (her birthday) to let her know how I have missed her and what I wish she could have lived to see and share. When my father died, almost twenty years ago, I began writing annual letters to him on his birthday as well. All these missives are kept in a few large journals that I go back through again and again. Although it wasn't part of my original intention, nowadays they serve as a reminder of many of the significant milestones in my life. Unlike many of my journals, which are meant to be private scribblings, these letters have been written in a way that I am comfortable sharing them with others. Someday I will even pass them on to my son.

Are you inspired to try your hand and heart at journaling? How might you begin? Is there someone to whom you might want to write a special letter?

How to Make the Most of
Your Journal Process

So, have I inspired you to start keeping a journal? Following are some basic prompts to get your journaling juices flowing.

What are three things you would like to accomplish within the next three months?

Complete the statement "I am ____" at least twenty times, writing down whatever comes to mind. Don't edit yourself. Let the words come. Allow yourself to even be surprised by what shows up. (A variation of this is the question, "Who do I say I am?" which may elicit different responses.)

Other sentence starters for exploration:

I am not	I would like
I will	I love
I will not	I will not tolerate

What advice would you give yourself at this time in your life?

Imagine you were interviewing YOU and answer the following questions:

- What five to ten major events and/or choices brought you to this point in your life?

- Looking back, what three things do you wish you had tried?

- If you had to choose an object/symbol that represented your past, what would it be?

- If you had to choose an object/symbol that represents the present, what would it be?

- If you had to choose an object/symbol that represents your future, what would it be?

- Consider this quote by David Viscott: *"The purpose of life is to discover your gift. The meaning of life is to give your gift away."* In what ways might this apply to your life?

Complete the following four exercises:

- List three internal changes you may need to make to live a more meaningful and joyful life.

- List three external changes you may need to make to live a more meaningful and joyful life.

- List three positive qualities that you feel are at the core of who you are.

- List three qualities that you would like to develop.

If you could try one to five new things over the next year what would they be?

MAKE LISTS

List-making can also be a revealing way to dive into self-exploration. To make it even more interesting, when you think your list is complete, ask yourself "and what else?" Here are some ideas to get you started:

1. Make a list of twenty-five things you love / appreciate about yourself.

Don't edit or judge your answers. Just write down everything that comes into your mind.

2. Alternately, make a list of your gifts (those things you were born with) and talents/skills (those things you have learned or enhanced through your own attention and discipline).

3. List twenty-five things that you do and/or would like to do that are fun / enjoyable / entertaining / stimulating.

4. Write down twenty-five things (or more—keep going till you've mind-dumped everything you can think of even if they sound petty or silly) that zap your energy or deplete you in some way. Choose one and write down three things you can do to eliminate / minimize this "toleration." This list can become a roadmap toward a more fulfilling life. So, jump into action and do what needs to be done, and then choose another zapper to tackle. Keep going until you have eliminated/minimized as many as possible and have strategized ways to cope with the rest.

5. Consider the possibility that everything that happens can teach you something. EVERYTHING! Think of a very challenging situation from the past or present and list all that you have learned / are learning from it.

6. Create a gratitude page. Write down three things you are grateful for in your life right now. Every day add something you are particularly and specifically grateful for that day.

TOUGH QUESTIONS

1. If you wanted to impart to your children—or the young people to whom you are close—the three most important things that you've learned in your life so far, what would they be?

2. What gives you the greatest joy, satisfaction, and renewal in your life? How can you do more of these things?

3. Think of someone you admire deeply (alive or dead) and list some reasons why. How can you access these qualities within yourself?

COMPLETE ANY/ALL OF THE FOLLOWING SENTENCES in as much detail *and* in as many ways as you would like. (Hint: there are multiple possibilities for each phrase. One way to do this exercise is to keep writing the first phrase and completing the sentence again and again until nothing more comes to mind.)

- I choose...

- I believe...

- I want to be...

- I want to have...

- I want to know / know about...

- I want to serve / contribute my gifts and talents to...

Things Are Not Always
What They Seem

"Things are not always what they seem; the first
appearance deceives many; the intelligence of a
few perceives what has been carefully hidden."

~FROM *THE PHAEDRUS* WRITTEN BY PLATO—
A DIALOGUE BETWEEN PLATO'S PROTAGONIST, SOCRATES, AND
PHAEDRUS, WHO MAY OR MAY NOT HAVE BEEN AN ACTUAL PERSON.

Were you ever misjudged as a child? I know that I was. Actually, my suspicion is that this is true for all of us, both as children and as adults. Others look at our behaviors and make assumptions through the lens of their individual beliefs, experiences, and understandings. We do the same with others. As a child I was judged to be a snob. This began because my mom was quite ill from the time I was very young, and so I spent a whole lot of sleepless nights, arriving at school tired and worried. Also, my tendency was to be a shy and serious child, perhaps for all sorts of reasons, perhaps because it is just how I was wired. I was, fortunately, a really good student who loved to learn and did well in school, so I sometimes received special attention from teachers. The bottom line is that I was thought to be aloof because I tended to be quiet and to not participate as often or as fully as I might have or as others did. It took years to find my path out of that particular way of being and being seen. Ah but there are always lessons to be learned in growing up and growing (b)older. The two, great big *AHAs!* for me from that time in my life were *don't live by the assumptions others make about you* and *don't make assumptions about others.* These ideas have not, by any means, been easy to learn and live by *and yet* they have served me well.

The end result is that we see things as we are, not as they are. There is no other way because we all filter incoming information based on what we already know. We all live within our own stories and constructs of reality. We scan all input to determine what it is most like/not like in order to process what we are encountering. Then our brain gets to work interpreting and judging everything and reacting or responding accordingly. That's why the adage "change your mind, change your life" makes such good sense.

Jumping to conclusions tends to win out over uncertainty and ongoing curiosity time after time. To make things even more difficult, we will look for evidence that supports what we want to believe and promote, often ignoring other facts and figures that would contradict our assumptions. Right now, as I am writing this, it is really cold outside. There are all sorts of frigid temperature records being broken in the eastern part of the United States and elsewhere. So those who don't believe in global warming are going HA! *If there's such a thing as global warming how could it be so cold?* But, actually, studies suggest that one factor could be the warming in the Arctic, which allows more frigid air to escape southward. Things may not always be what they seem.

Back in the 1970s I took a series of workshops in Silva Mind Control. José Silva claimed to have developed a program that trained people to enter certain brain states of enhanced awareness. He originally developed the course to help his own children do better in school. The method uses guided imagery techniques to shift negative programing so that, with practice, students can realize their potential and reach their goals. Honestly, I don't remember much about the program except that I found value in learning how to scrutinize my thoughts, beliefs, and opinions more carefully to determine their source. From that vantage point I could better evaluate their accuracy as well as how those thoughts served *or didn't serve* me. My biggest take-away was about noticing all the ways my brain forms judgments—like/don't like, good/

bad, interesting/not interesting, beautiful/ugly—about just about everything. We were taught, whenever a judgmental thought came into our heads, to immediately label it "Judging! Judging!" to ourselves so that we could look beyond our immediate prejudices and develop a more considered understanding of all that we encounter. To this day, when I catch myself being closed-minded or critical, the words "Judging! Judging!" simply pop into my head. It's rather fascinating to pay attention to just how much we evaluate and appraise constantly. Try it and see what happens.

Years ago, I had a really telling experience. I was sitting in a lovely fancy hotel dining room in Bologna, Italy having lunch. Seated two tables away was a beautiful woman who actually spent the entire meal putting on make-up with a really big mirror in her hand. I was appalled and had lots to say about her to my husband. Then later, when we were walking around, there she was doing a modeling shoot on the hotel grounds for a brochure. Shame on me. I could feel myself blushing crimson. That incident happened almost fifty years ago, and I am still reminded of it when a *Judging-Judging* moment comes along.

One of the cleverest book titles I ever heard was *What You Think of Me is None of My Business* by Terry Cole-Whittaker. Doesn't that say it all? How often do we become concerned or even immobilized by the negative opinions of others? Actually, even flattery and compliments can sabotage us if we hang on to someone's every word for affirmation as to who we are and what we are doing.

Given that things are not always what they seem what can we do to stay unguarded and expansive in order to most generously and generatively view ourselves and each other? The image of those nested Russian dolls I remember playing with as a child comes to mind. What was most delightful about receiving them was that the gift was so much more than it first appeared to be. Inside the biggest doll there was tucked away a slightly smaller one and then an even smaller one within that one, all the way to the tiniest doll hidden within six or eight or ten others. Symbolically, this can represent the progression of getting to the core of who we really are by shedding multiple layers of outer appearances. We can do the reverse, too, starting with the tiniest doll and, piece by piece, seeing her step into fuller and grander versions of herself. Neither of these interpretations is the Truth and both give us something to think about and perhaps move toward.

Becoming a Mama Bear

"Bless those who challenge us to grow, to stretch, to move
beyond the knowable, to come back home to our elemental and
essential nature. Bless those who challenge us for they remind
us of doors we have closed and doors we have yet to open."

~Navajo prayer

My totem—or good luck charm or favorite symbol (call it what you will)—is a she-bear. This is not something I chose but rather something that chose me. I know this because at some point in time I had been gifted with so many bears—made of wood or stone or crystal or porcelain or clay—that I began to take notice. So, I did a bit of research and discovered that, according to Native American Indian lore, a she-bear is the great maternal protectrice, defiant and strong, who heals using nature's ways. *AHA!* That would be me.

These bears began appearing in my life around the same time that I came face to face with the most unexpected, significant, and scary challenges of my life. From the time he was young, my son Reid was plagued with severe and debilitating asthma that took a toll on his health. There were lots of frightening emergency trips to the hospital, and he required constant allergy shots and medications, some with long-term side effects.

The thought of saddling Reid for life with the consequences of these drugs was terrifying. I felt helpless, frightened, and desperate. In addition, as he grew older, Reid's activities became more and more restricted. By the time he was ten, he couldn't play sports at school and sometimes couldn't even walk around the block without getting out of breath and wheezing. So, I began to study everything that I could lay my hands on about alternative approaches to health and healing. As I learned more and more, I worked with Reid to end his dependence on any medications at all. It was definitely a joint effort because Reid had to be willing to adhere to all the new-fangled ideas I was suggesting. We began to meditate together, and, when his chest felt "tight," we practiced sitting quietly and imagining that we were breathing in the color blue, because in color therapy it is considered a calming color. We explored lots of other healing practices as well including yoga, pranayama breathing, herbs, folk remedies, ginger compresses, kinesiology, shiatsu, affirmations, and visualization.

In spite of his doctor's skepticism and warnings, Reid and I persevered. It is hard to explain how frightening it is to literally take responsibility for your child's life. The doctors said I was foolish and imprudent. I responded by taking a CPR course, learning crisis breathing techniques from an emergency room nurse, and keeping strong allergy medicines (which fortunately I never had to use) handy. I had turned into a fierce and dedicated mama bear. My husband and I had a steam unit built into our bathroom (which required running a separate electrical line from the basement to our fifth-floor apartment!). In that moist warm air infused with herbs Reid was able to breathe more easily when in a crisis. I also prayed a lot.

Every night Reid and I would march around in a bathtub filled with ice water to strengthen our immune systems (a suggestion from my mentor, Annemarie Colbin—whom you will "meet" in the next paragraph—based on her childhood practice of running around barefoot in the snow in Norway). The deal was that while in that frigid water we could shout out all sorts of curse words but the moment our toes touched the floor again we had to stop. That way we stayed *laughterfully* distracted. We also worked out together, jumping on a small at-home trampoline every day to build up lung capacity. I held firmly to the belief that in six months Reid would be strong and healthy enough for us to run one and a quarter miles around the New York City reservoir together. We kept a wall calendar and checked off each day. At the end of six months, we achieved that goal…and more.

Along with everything else we were doing, we began to focus on eating more healthfully. We cooked together and giggled and grimaced at some of the early concoctions we tossed into the garbage on my quest to understanding whole foods and how to make them taste delicious and satisfying. But we got better at it. I concentrated intensely on the impact that food choices could have on health in general and allergies in particular. The blessing and the real turning of the tides came when I came across a flyer in a small neighborhood health food store advertising a course in healthy cooking at a school called Natural Gourmet run by Annemarie Colbin. The little intuitive voice inside me urged me to take that course, even though I already knew a lot about cooking. That course changed the course of my life…and Reid's.

Over the next six months, in large measure due to the tutelage and guidance of Annemarie, Reid was weaned off all medication and there had not been a single emergency run to the hospital for an adrenaline shot. He was able to begin to actively participate in many of the activities that he yearned to do—swimming, squash, tennis, and belonging to a boy's athletic club that met on Saturdays for team sports. My own life and sense of well-being also changed as I focused on health-wise food choices that nurtured my body, mind, and spirit.

Another Story: Reid had already been on this nutritious but somewhat restrictive diet for six months with profound positive results. Summer was coming, and he wanted to go to camp. I was very reluctant about exposing him to normal camp fare after the progress we had made. The situation seemed impossible. But he had been so cooperative about so many limitations and constraints for so long that I was determined not to disappoint him. I looked at what it would take to send him, and I just did it. I made arrangements with the camp director and, using their daily menu plans as a guide, I created recipes, cooked, froze, and shipped all healthy meals plus daily snacks and treats for the summer. I paid the camp cooks extra to heat Reid's special meals and make him fresh salads and vegetables every day. I located a health store sixty miles away that delivered bottled, all-natural, sugar free juices during the summer. My hard work and Reid's own determination to help himself get well paid off and he remained free of any medications all summer. I continued to prepare meals for the next two summers, doubling my production so that another boy with asthma could attend the same camp. I know this sounds heroic, and perhaps it was, but what I want to make clear is how much of my motivation came from fear and the anguish of having a son who was so ill. I had to try. Such are the responsibilities of a mama bear.

All of these actions and activities ultimately led to a change in focus and direction as I experienced two big *AHAs!* First, I didn't have to be an impotent victim in the face of illness and life crises. I had choices. There were things I could do and there were people I could go to for help and support. Second, the more I pursued this healing path the more the universe "provided" in the form of teachers, guides, information, and opportunities. Soon, friends and mothers started calling me for advice. I returned to school to earn a certificate in nutrition. I started a counseling practice. Also, because of my extensive background and training in the culinary arts as well as my growing experience with food for healing, I was invited to teach vegetarian cooking for Natural Gourmet and to participate in the writing of a cookbook by that name. When I first moved to Florida, I continued to be involved with sharing my love of healthy cooking through planning and cooking for several large events as well as lecturing on how food and lifestyle choices affect our well-being. All these years later, I remain committed to eating mindfully and encourage my son and grandchildren to do the same.

By the way, I continue to surround myself with bear totems as well as teddy bears (because for me they represent the other side of a she-bear's make-up—the loving and cuddly side). They have taken up residency throughout my home as a potent reminder of what is possible, especially if a mama bear feels that there is a threat to her offspring!

In what ways might the concept of being/becoming a Mama (or Papa) Bear resonate with you? Consider the ways you have and continue to step up and speak out for someone or something that matters to you. Is there some next person or idea worthy of awakening you inner Mama/Papa Bear?

The World Is in Too Much Trouble to Make Ourselves Small

"Life shrinks or expands in proportion to one's courage."

~ANAIS NIN, DIARIST, ESSAYIST, NOVELIST, SHORT STORY WRITER

Many years ago, nutritionist, cooking teacher, and author Anne-marie Colbin gave me my first opportunity to teach about healthy food and its preparation at Natural Gourmet in New York City. In the previous chapter on *Becoming a Mama Bear*, I mention that I took her classes, not because I didn't know how to cook, but because I was on a quest to find out about healthy and nutritious food and the difference it could make in my own life and that of my family. After the first class, Annemarie asked me, "What are you doing here? You know too much to be in a beginner cooking class." I explained that, yes, I had grown up around good food and loved to cook, but my motivation was to find a way to support my son Reid in getting stronger and dealing more effectively with his asthma. I wanted to see if changing his diet could make a difference. I shared with Annemarie what I was already doing, both in terms of foods and other healing modalities and practices. She made several important suggestions. That day I purchased her *Book of Whole Meals* and proceeded to cook through it from front to back, trying out every recipe. It was a thirty-day meal plan and included recipes for breakfast, lunch, and dinner. What happened was that in those next thirty days, with the addition of this revised diet, Reid was weaned off his steroidal inhalant. It felt like an amazing triumph and inspired me to want to learn more...much more. So, I continued taking classes and experimenting.

Somewhere along the line I invited Annemarie to my home for dinner. I had grown up in the restaurant business in New York and had studied with many great chef-teachers, both in the city and abroad. Over the years I had become quite an accomplished cook. I remember distinctly what unfolded after dinner as if it were yesterday. Annemarie came up to me and said, "You *really* can cook. I've decided that you are going to teach for me." My first reaction was pure fear. I told her that I didn't know enough, that I wasn't good enough, not to mention that I was terrified of standing up in front of people and speaking. She looked at me and said something I have never forgotten, one of the biggest *AHA! moments* of my life, words I have carried with me always. She looked at me and said, *"The world is in too much trouble for you to make yourself small."* She insisted that, because I obviously know what I know, it was absolutely essential that I share this gift with others. That's how I began to teach cooking…and more. To this day, those words, more than any others, give me the impetus and courage to put myself out there, give voice to what I know as well as attempt new things, pick myself up when I make a mistake, dust myself off, and move beyond my fears and self-imposed limitations.

Over the course of my lifetime, I have dared to stretch beyond my comfort zone again and again. I went back to school, first to become a nutritionist and then, years later, to become a life coach. I worked hard at finding ways to communicate my knowledge and convictions about choosing to live in the healthiest and most fulfilling way possible. I further challenged myself by doing lots of public speaking. I figured that if I could learn to speak in front of thirty students while making a full and elaborate lunch or dinner for them, standing up and standing (more or less) still and just speaking should be a cinch. It wasn't, but step by step I learned. Mostly, I needed to remind myself that it wasn't about me or what people thought about my "performance." I believed that I had important and relevant things to share. I just had to move beyond my own natural shyness in order to let my enthusiasm and my passion shine through.

One day I took a different kind of leap of faith and began to publicly share my poetry, which I had kept hidden in a shoe box until then. Since that personally courageous breakthrough, I have self-published four books, have had two more books that include poetry published by Blue Mountain Arts, and my poems have been included in anthologies as well as in the books of others. I've taken on leadership roles that were a real reach and stretch for me and then did whatever I needed to do to get the job done well. To this day, every time I reach and stretch, I inwardly thank Annemarie with all my heart for that unexpected jump-start into a brave new way of being and doing which I didn't think I was capable of handling.

When we enter into the wisdom years, it becomes more apparent than ever that the world is in too much trouble for any of us to shrink back and not offer our sagacity. The world needs our ideas, our words, our gifts, our talents, and our willingness to be fully involved in our communities. We know what we know, and the world benefits from all that we have discovered over the years.

I still suffer from what I label as the I-don't-know-enough syndrome. I am aware that I am not the only one. I don't know why this is so. But I have befriended enough people and coached enough clients to recognize that we all have these nasty little voices in our heads whispering about our not-good-enoughness. Still, at some point, we each need to come to terms with that inner chattering. We each need to stop thinking that someday maybe we will finally be (smart, informed, intelligent, talented) enough. I had to learn to let go of my ongoing belief that when I read one more book, go to one more lecture, or take one more course, then I will finally know enough to be worthy of sharing both information gleaned and my perspective. Life is a share-as-we-go journey. Something else I learned from Annemarie is that, "We teach what we want to learn." If we really want to learn, do, and be more, it is essential to step way out of our comfy corners and—thank you Nike for this brilliant catchphrase—just do it, gaining expertise and skill as we go.

In his beautiful and moving book, *The River,* author Michael Neale talks about the place where we each confront our grief and fear in order to step into the fullness of our life and purpose. "The River" is the place where we finally stop playing small. There comes a time, actually many times, when it is quite simply my turn—or yours—to jump into the great big river of life, to play the music or to sing the song or to make a joyful noise that can be heard loud and clear. Sometimes it is without a doubt my time—or yours—to take a stance or a stand or maybe just jump up and be the first to dance or to confront a naysayer or to applaud. Years ago, I went to hear Buckminster Fuller speak. His talk was brilliant, and at the end I wanted to jump to my feet and clap loudly to show my appreciation. But no one else was getting up, and so I stayed demurely seated. After the modest applause stopped, he remarked that perhaps he had not done such a good job in presenting his ideas this time because usually he is rewarded with a standing ovation. I had so wanted to stand up, but my discomfort held me back. I vowed then and there that I would never not be the first person to stand up and cheer when there was something or someone worth cheering about or for. Again and again, I am learning to step up and step out of my comfort zone and claim my place at the top or in the circle—or wherever life is beckoning me to show up. My hope is that by sharing my stories I am encouraging you to do the same.

By the way, a corollary to all this is that I've learned that I cannot simply wait to be discovered. I have to be willing to talk about what I have done and created as well as what I am capable of doing and creating. We need to do what it takes so that people can find us, give us or ask for our guidance, and hire us or put us in front of the right audience. I have been an entrepreneur for a very long time, and my biggest discomfort has always been marketing and promoting myself. It has required a whole lot of boldness for me to take steps to make it over that particular hurdle. Through the years I have also become clever enough to hire various public relations experts, marketing gurus, and savvy social media specialists to promote me and what in the world I do.

I've learned that to live fully and courageously, my gaze must shift to something bigger. I have to move past the thought that it is all about me. Annemarie taught me to go into the tiny bathroom at the cooking school before each class and go through a ritual of leaving my ego there, high up on a shelf, offering my *ego-self* assurances that I would come back to retrieve her after class. If what we know and what we have to share are to come through us and make a difference in the lives of others, we cannot be worried about how we look or what people think about us. We have to become focused on something larger and more significant than just ourselves, something more purposeful and meaningful. We must each remember that it's not about ME. It's about how we can serve.

Is there some way you have perhaps allowed yourself to stay small? How might you now choose step into your most courageous self?

Your Confidence Is Showing

"People become really quite remarkable when they start thinking that they can do things. When they believe in themselves they have the first secret of success."
~NORMAN VINCENT PEALE,
AMERICAN MINISTER AND AUTHOR

The way you walk into a room, the look on your face, the twinkle in your eye, the manner in which you stand up tall, and how you engage with others—these are all subtle cues about your confidence level. Your projection of confidence is often what lands you the assignment or gets the job done or opens doors that would have stayed slammed shut. I learned all of this the hard way. I was not a particularly confident child. Never mind the reasons. I was shy and not very sure of myself, which is always a particularly difficult combo. I might have stayed that way had life not conspired to push me into finding my voice. It started when my son was so sick, and I had to become a Mama Bear for his sake as well as mine. Then I was challenged to build my confidence because of Annemarie Colbin's insistence that I teach at her school.

Though I have shared those stories, there's more to share because when the going gets tough, it can be tough to access that strong, resilient, and positive aspect of ourselves. That's when we need to somehow dig deep and find the inner resources to regain our composure and conviction or, at least, act *as if* we have it all together…until we do.

Consider the expression "fake it till you make it." On the one hand, the idea of *faking it* sounds phony and disingenuous. Most people, to the best of their ability, want to be authentic and real. They don't appreciate it when others put on airs, and so it's not something they aspire to do themselves. But sometimes real courage is the ability to step into the fray or onto the playing fields of life not only with grit and gusto, but also with a bit of bravado. For me the *AHA!* happened when I finally understood that it's more about accessing the courageous part that lives deep within me than about just pretending. If you believe that what you stand up for is worth it, and that being confident, clear, and fervent about your choice and message make a difference, then your motivation to meet obstacles head-on (no matter the hidden tremor in your limbs or your voice) is what matters most. Even if the storm or disaster never materializes, you will emerge the better for having arrived with dignity and well-prepared.

Research demonstrates that striking a pose of assurance will actually help you access that part of yourself. So next time you need to show confidence, experiment by tapping into your inner Wonder Woman or channeling your superhero. Take a stand with your hands on your hips and your feet planted firmly on the ground so as to convey to your body and brain a clear message about your willpower and resolve. One research experiment concluded that sitting like a boss with your feet up on your desk will access that powerful feeling of being in control and capable of making important decisions. Ever since learning about all this posing and posturing, I have been playing around with it, exaggerating it, hamming it up (if only for myself). IT WORKS. I promise.

Here's another important strategy—walk before you fly. Any pilot taking off on their first solo flight can testify to the racing heart, sweaty palms, hyper-focused attention, and endless badgering by their inner scaredy-cat. It takes grit and grace to pull it off safely and countless months of practice to gain the skills and expertise necessary. Pilots rack up many hours of training before they take the controls. Like a pilot, you're going to have to first earn your wings if you ever want to soar. But unlike learning to fly, learning to be confident is an ongoing process—one that begins again and again with each new possibility.

While well-meaning friends may tell you to "just do it," in truth, developing confidence takes a while. Each time you reach higher, each time you fall short, each time it becomes apparent that you must hone your skills to some sharper level, you need to be willing to take that step. But first you need to get your head on straight, get in touch with what your heart has to teach you, and set some sensible ground rules. The last thing you want to do is set yourself up for a fall. It's not that you have to do everything perfectly or you'll crash, it's that you need to have some well-thought-out procedures in place in order to progress at an intelligent and sustainable pace and avoid disaster.

When I was in my thirties, I went through some tough times in my life and needed an outlet, not just for the sake of my well-being, but also for the sake of my sanity. Someone suggested jogging. I was, however, not a particularly natural or strong athlete. So, I started small... walking, then running a mile or two a few days a week. Progress was erratic at first, and I never even dreamed that one day I would develop the strength and stamina to be able to run a marathon. But, slowly and surely, step by step, I got better. Year after year, I kept at it. Then someone asked me to join them in a 5K race...and then a 10K. Next came a half marathon and finally, a full-blown New York City marathon, as part of the Central Park team no less. With sweaty palms and some trepidations about whether I would let the team down, I said "yes." It was glorious! What I remember best about that magical time was when I knew in my gut that I had found my stride and the improbable had become possible. I completed that first run in under five hours and the next one, a year later, in under four and a half, which, considering I was in my forties by then, felt like quite an accomplishment. I still have the certificates hanging on my office wall to keep encouraging my *can-do* attitude.

A final strategy worth trying—re-vision yourself. We each hold a gallery of pictures in our mind's eye that is a reflection of what we think and feel about ourselves. These images are not accurate representations, but rather a complex portrayal of how we see ourselves through the filter of our experiences, beliefs, and estimations. They include an accumulation of both our past impressions and our future projections. Unfortunately, instead of choosing to see ourselves in our best light, all too often we examine ourselves through a magnifying glass that exaggerates our perceived faults and shortcomings. All too often we default to our supposed failures and forget to acknowledge and celebrate our best selves. We may also suffer from *comparisonitis* and, rather than focus on our magnificent uniqueness, we pay attention instead to all the ways we believe we don't measure up to someone else or to some illusive and imaginary yardstick.

The best remedy for all this negativity is to first focus, with both kindness and clarity, on who and how you choose to be. Then do everything possible to move toward and step into, embody, or emulate that envisioned persona. It's about both re-visioning and revising, about seeing yourself whole and authentic, and appreciating the one-of-a-kind gift that you are in the world. It's also about making the important changes that allow your best Self to shine through.

Public speaking had always been a big challenge for me until my dear friend and fabulous speaker/presentation coach Temple Hayes gave me this tip which became the *AHA!* I needed to seriously own my voice. Before stepping onto the stage and up to the microphone, pay attention to your limiting beliefs about the *small you with your small worries* sitting in the wings or in the chair waiting to be announced. Realize that you, and what you have to share, are bigger than that. Recognize that what you have to say, and your unique way of saying it, are important. Imagine yourself shedding or leaving behind that smallness as you stand up. Then imagine wrapping yourself in a luminous cloak of your own brilliance, passion, and authenticity. With that image in mind, step up to the podium with poise and presence and begin. Sounds a bit way out there, but I have to say, it works every time.

Part of any re-visioning process, of course, requires that you actually do what it takes to polish up your appearance until you beam. At the same time, no amount of outward attention will matter if you don't simultaneously practice showing up in your own mind the way you want to be seen in the world—strong and sassy, calm and confident, poised and prepared, graceful and gracious, and kind and collaborative. This is not an exercise in self-deception. Rather, it is the process of creating and developing your true Self from the inside out. It requires *seeing* within you what you are striving to bring forth, and then embracing and living up to and into that image. To quote Wayne Dyer, "You'll see it when you believe it."

What do you want to see now? Visualization is a terrific tool for strengthening this ability. It is not about just playing around with impossibilities; it is a practice for calling forth possibilities from the ethers of your imagination. Try this for starters: Every morning, take just a few minutes to imagine your best self, glowing with health and vitality, stepping out into the world to meet the day. Hold that charismatic person with great care and tenderness on the inner screen of your mind for a while, and then release that person the same way you would a wish or a prayer into the limitlessness of the universe. Pay attention to what happens.

The Practice of Yoga

tadāsana
*mountain pose**

feet firmly
grounded in the earth
resting reverently
on the belly of
the Great Mother...
with reverence
I dedicate my practice
to all that is

When it comes to yoga, *practice* is the operative word. Unlike so many sports and exercise regimens where there are measurable goals and outcomes, yoga is above all a commitment to show up and step onto one's mat with the *heartful* intention to be wholly attentive to oneself. Yes, of course, the more I practice, the stronger, more flexible, and increasingly balanced I become. But the goal is not actually about quantifiable "improvements." Rather the focus of yoga is ultimately the capacity to simply be fully present to whatever is showing up in my body, mind, and spirit in the moment.

---

* Minx Boren, *Feeling My Way—99 Poetic Journeys*, (Palm Beach Gardens, FL: Fourfold Path Inc., 2008): Page 136.

I started practicing yoga almost fifty years ago because I was diagnosed with a severe and painful scoliosis. As part of a last-ditch attempt to avoid two spinal fusions, I chose to attend a neighborhood yoga class. I am not exaggerating when I say that this exploration into the whole realm of mindful movement, mindful breathing, and mindful presence changed my life. Not only did I avoid surgery, but my entire perspective about LIFE changed through this practice. There have been so many *AHA! moments* while engaged in the practice that I hardly know where to begin nor which ones to include. What I will say to create a context for the following top eight points is that as it is in yoga and on the mat, so it is in life.

Just keep breathing.

Let's start with the breath, the most basic and crucial element of any practice. No matter what is being taught or demonstrated, no matter which way I am attending to and moving my body, the most important thing I can do is to just keep breathing. (I actually have a T-shirt created by one of my teachers with those words printed on it as a poignant and practical reminder.) The central question, in each position held or in any flow sequence, remains the same—*where is my breath?* The first focus is always how to remain conscious of the breath, how to breathe into the pose, and how to expand at every level to receive and then release one breath at a time. The same holds true in life. No matter what we are doing or dealing with, the breath is the constant anchor that we can return to again and again in order to stay centered and focused on the task at hand.

Comparisonitis is a trap and a distraction.

Yoga is neither a contest nor a performance. It is an opportunity to practice being present to one's own body, mind, and spirit—one breath at a time, one movement at a time. It doesn't matter who else is in the class or what the instructor is able to demonstrate. All that matters are how lovingly and patiently you are willing to work with your own whole Self. To take it to the next level, yoga is not even about competing with yourself—with your own last best "performance." I remember one of my teachers saying to me, while I was doing a forward bend and working really hard to stretch far enough to get my hands flat on the floor, that "there is no enlightenment to be found when you finally reach the ground. There is only the next breath…and then the next." Isn't this also true in life? One of the hardest lessons we each must learn is to simply do and be our best, whatever that means in the moment at hand. A job well executed, like a yoga practice session well done, is one where we can feel satisfied that we did what we were capable of just then…with joy and gratitude.

Every day is unique.

Just because you could do a headstand effortlessly or stay balanced in tree pose for more than a minute on Monday doesn't mean that Tuesday's practice will yield the same outcome. In each moment what matters is that we are receptive to what is going on, to the ongoing shifts and changes that happen within ourselves. Any expectation sets us up for failure. The result is that, rather than a sense of delight and of well-being, anything less than what we intend for ourselves becomes a disappointment. This perception is also just as true in life as it is on the mat. When we step into our day free of "shoulds" and endless demands on ourselves, we free ourselves to participate fully in whatever is happening right then and there. When I can be just here, just now, just open to the way things are unfolding and just willing to be with what's so, my energy, enthusiasm, and gratitude all increase exponentially. It is then that my joy becomes real and palpable.

There are lots of variations and all are good.

Fortunately, the practice of yoga has been around for centuries, and so we are the beneficiaries of the wisdom of the ages. Nowhere is this more apparent than when learning the steps or *kramas* of a pose. I say steps rather than levels because wherever we are on the path to our own fullest expression of the pose is the perfect place for us to be. For example, while doing *tree pose,* one foot is rooted on the ground while the other foot can progressively move from toes on the floor/sole of foot against the ankle to sole of foot pressed against the middle of the lower leg or upper thigh. One hand can hold a bar or both hands can be pressed together in prayer at the sternum or one or both hands can reach to the sky in a full extension of one's "branches." Tree pose can be done with or without props to help steady us. Wherever we are in our practice, we are still reaping the benefits of the pose, and we are still reminded to breathe in and out and to stay present. Once again this is an *AHA!* that has served me well. Whatever I am up to, wherever I am in an experience or endeavor, it is all good. There is no one right answer or right way. If I can remain unattached to any particular outcome, then I can celebrate whatever variation I am experiencing right here and right now. The ramifications of this idea are endless, freeing, and expansive.

Balance isn't static.

Speaking of tree pose, I am reminded of the whole idea of balance and how it is presented through yoga teachings. Balance is never about holding tightly or tensing every muscle in order to maintain equilibrium. Rather, it is quite the opposite. The surest way to fall is to try too hard and rigidly to make something happen. Only when we can soften into the pose and become quietly present to our own center can we find our way to ease and balance. A recent *AHA!* occurred at a weekend retreat. Rodney Yee, while teaching a particular balancing pose, actually encouraged us to be willing to topple and fall...to actually experiment with what it would feel like to be that relaxed and playful rather than concerned with "performance" and looking good. Because he urged us to give ourselves permission to investigate the space and spaciousness of the pose, I found myself truly enjoying the experience rather than trying so hard to stay upright and look "perfect." For someone with bilateral hip replacements (which make it rather challenging for me to balance in the first place), this was quite a revelation. As in yoga, so it is in life. I am asking myself, *where can I loosen up and allow myself to open up to being more playful, joyful, accepting, and, dare I say, fearless?*

Showing up matters.

On my own, I will sometimes put down my mat and do some yoga poses for fifteen to fifty minutes, depending on the day and what else is going on. This allows me to stay limber and also serves as a ritual gesture to affirm my commitment to my practice. It's about showing up day after day. I still show up to take yoga classes at least three times a week, choosing different teachers so that I can reap the benefits of their individual expertise, style, and wisdom. Another reason to show up for class is that there is a certain vibe in the room that comes from being part of a collective energy. The correlation to LIFE is obvious. Showing up is a statement of commitment. Participating with others who are also committed to being fully present, doing their best, and bringing their best self to the moment or project can make all the difference in the quality of the experience as well as the outcomes.

The order of things matters.

Until recently, when I have practiced on my own, I would generally either do some random poses—whatever popped into my head, creating my own flow as I go for as long as I am in the mood or have time for—or I do the Bikram twenty-six pose sequence because I happen to know it by heart. Then I had another *AHA!* experience in that same class given by Colleen and Rodney Yee. I learned that there is a method and exactness that goes into the planning of their classes. Colleen is the author of *Yoga for Life*, which I refer to when practicing on my own. The sequences in the book reflect an understanding about how various flows impact the body as well as the mind. There are fourteen sequences that she shares, including a specific sequence designed for each of the following: dealing with trauma, building confidence, awakening, and dealing with chaos. And so it is in life. First of all, there is no one answer to all situations. Nor is it likely that we will achieve our best outcomes if we go about working in a haphazard manner—whether we are focused on troublesome issues or worthy goals. Having a good plan and clear guidelines based on intelligent reasoning and good intuitive understanding definitely can help.

Integration

Every yoga practice ends with *shavasana*—the Sanskrit word for corpse pose. This is the moment when, having given our best effort, we get to relax, recline, and let go. Treating a yoga class like a workout and racing out the door after the sweaty part is over is actually cheating oneself of the true benefits. Our body needs time to integrate all that we have explored and practiced. The final moments of a class always include an opportunity to lie down and just breathe, allowing our body to surrender and completely let go. Interestingly, this correlates to what brain science tells us. The best way to commit something to memory is to get a good night's sleep. Whether learning a vocabulary list, a new language, a scientific formula or a tennis stroke, we *spindle* our learning to long-term memory when we sleep on it. Perhaps *shavasana* is the yogic equivalent of a good night sleep. In any case, after spending time in *shavasana,* the very last ritual of a yoga class is to return to a seated position and, with hands prayerfully at heart center, bow and together utter the Sanskrit word "*namaste*," which is a gesture that honors both the sacredness of our practice and the divinity and perfection within each of us.

Yoga is an act of commitment to oneself. It is a private declaration to show up in full integrity and in full acceptance of oneself—both one's strengths and limitations—and simply work with what is. The key thoughts are grace, gratitude, focus, humor, and humility...thoughts that also serve us well in life in general.

Happy Mess!

no matter the chaos, the clutter, the fuss
there is joy to be found
in the happy messes of life
if only we allow our hearts
to smile and embrace the wholeness
and holiness of it all

My husband Mel and I have a favorite toast. Whenever we are having wine with dinner, we raise our glasses and clink them in a toast to "*happiness.*" When our son Reid was about four years old, we were all out sharing a family meal one evening when he decided to raise his glass (filled with juice) to toast with us. What was so adorable, and revealing, was that the words that came out of his mouth were "*happy mess.*" I was about to correct him when I stopped myself, realizing that his toast was absolutely perfect. If we could learn to accept and live with—maybe even celebrate—all the inevitable *happy messes* along the road of life, we would be well on our way to enjoying a wonderful life. *AHA!* indeed.

What very young children, and those of us who have learned a bit along life's journey, know is that things do not need to be perfect or pristine for joy to be present. As Martha Washington explained, "I have learned from experience that the greater part of our happiness or misery depends on our dispositions and not on our circumstances." Perhaps the whole point of life is simply to seek the happiness and fullness to be found moment by precious moment, no matter what's going on.

Here's another lesson learned by living. Life happens…and not always according to our best theories, ideas, and strategies. In fact, it mostly does *not* quite happen according to plan—or at least not according to our carefully laid out agendas, schedules, and lists. What we learn to recognize as we grapple and grow is that the most powerful *happiness strategy* in our human tool box is our capacity to apply thoughtful consideration, perspective, and compassion to whatever is happening when life is not going according to *our* idea of how it *should* be. By doing so, we reframe whatever is taking place in the most positive and inspiring ways possible.

I love Mark Twain's suggestion to "Give every day the chance to become the most beautiful of your life." Now there's an idea capable of creating a profound shift. *What would it be like to approach each new day as anything but ho-hum?* My cousin-brother Howie and I used to go for hikes in the woods around Chappaqua, New York. He had the delightful capacity to stop mid-step or mid-sentence and absolutely revel at the sun coming through the canopy of leaves and shining on the tree barks…or the bird hidden in the branches singing his heart out. Each experience of beauty would be, in that moment, the most startling and wondrous moment ever because we were fully present in it. I treasured those walks and am forever grateful to him for the *eyes wide open to wonder* perspective he instilled in me. Life didn't have to be perfect for the moment to be *AWEsome.* As a matter of fact, often one or the other or both of us were puzzling our way through some challenge or another, including life-threatening ones. It didn't matter. There are still *happy mess moments* to be found.

Those who have active children and/or pets witness this whole idea at a gut level. My coach friend Doug Autenrieth, a martial arts black belt who models discipline and the value of exquisitely high standards, absolutely embraced the whole *happy mess* concept when I shared it at a conference we were attending. Now he regales me with *happy mess moments* that his children are adding to the daily chaos of their now life. As he observes, "Life is good! We are living life as the *happy mess* that it is." *So how can we each do that?* I believe that the bottom line is that it is mostly about going with the flow…rather than sinking under the weight of the inevitable challenges inherent in living in the world instead of at a pristine retreat on a mountaintop. I remember hearing a devout leader making the observation that, if you truly want to practice living a spiritual life, give up on the idea that the best way to do so is to live in a quiet sanctuary. Instead, choose to spend your life in the whole muddled business of being in relationship with others. As Ralph Waldo Emerson said, "We may search the world over for joy but unless we carry it within us, we will not find it."

As we grow with gratitude, gusto, grit, and grace we finally come to understand this in our bones. There is a lovely story I have heard told about an elderly woman being moved into a nursing home. When she and her family arrived at the place, she declared, "I absolutely LOVE it here." Her daughter asked, "How can you know when you haven't even been inside yet?" Her wise mother replied, "Because I have already decided that I am going to!" Now there's an attitude I want to emulate if the time comes for me to move on from my current familiar comforts. I do believe that, time and again, it is up to us to decide how much responsibility we are willing to take for the joy in our life.

Happiness matters. I believe that our personal happiness (yours and mine) adds to the joy of the world, tilting the scales, however minutely, one person at a time, toward a more blissful world for all.

In the end, the questions become…*How much joy do you carry within you? How disposed are you to happiness? How much can/do you celebrate the happy messes? How are you creating joy along the way?*

Here's yet another aspect of the whole happy mess conundrum— stretching to the next level by actually embracing failure. I first heard Boston Philharmonic conductor Ben Zander speak at an International Coach Federation Conference many years ago. I was a newbie coach back then and wanted to belong, be smart, do things right and, above all, not open my mouth just to utter some particularly naïve question or observation. So, mostly I stayed quiet. As I soon found out, thanks to Ben Zander's exciting presentation, playing small was a BIG mistake.

Being a certifiable perfectionist, I respect the challenge of celebrating failures. Since the alternative is a whole lot of frustration and suffering, it's definitely been worth my while to practice embracing all the mistakes and goof-ups and "I can't believe I did/said/wrote THAT" embarrassments I have managed to stumble through on my way to whatever measures of success I have achieved. Ben Zander and Rosamund Stone Zander, in their book *The Art of Possibility: Transforming Professional and Personal Life,* write about his two best strategies for getting his already technically proficient students at the conservatory to be willing to risk making mistakes in order to find the magnificent passion embedded within the musical notes on the score. First, he gives every student an A grade in advance, as long as they show up and stay the course. Next, he requires that, whenever they fumble, they must raise their hands into the air and shout out "How fascinating!" This was a delightful *AHA!* for me, as well as for his students, I'm sure, because it allowed them to recognize that, to be brilliant, they must reach beyond their assumed competence to a greater capacity for self-expression. Imagine what you might be willing to risk if you already knew you would receive an A. Imagine the liberation that could come from being fascinated by the necessary fumbles along the way to accomplishing something more. Thanks to Zander's advice, I have learned, as a motivational speaker, to not agonize about the mistakes and bloopers of a particular presentation. Rather, I do a reframe and recognize how my mind sometimes does its own thing and fails to follow what my brain has memorized. I will actually say "How fascinating!" while presenting and let my audience know how I have missed the mark. It's a great way to keep things real.

Remember that failures can be fruitful, and maybe even fun/funny, if we are willing to be feisty, flamboyant, fabulous, and fearless. The story goes that Thomas Edison failed more than a thousand times while trying to create the lightbulb. When asked about it, Edison allegedly responded that he had not failed. Rather he had discovered a thousand ways to *not* make a lightbulb. How's that for a terrific tweak in the right direction? *Can you think of a tweak of your own with making?*

Honor Your Lineage

*two crones**

my grandmother was a modern woman
left the old country and the old ways behind
and taught me to play gin rummy and go fish…

my bubbie was an ancient woman
of another time and place
a reluctant refugee who sang old songs with strange words…

from one I came to understand
the promise of the future
from the other the sacredness of the past

We all arrive here on earth from somewhere—from what perhaps may best be called *the great mystery*—and are received into the arms of those who are here awaiting our arrival. Beyond this first wave of welcomers, there are also all of those who have come before them… and before them. We each stand on the shoulders of others—many others. One of the most significant *AHA! moments* of my life happened many years ago when I was invited to participate in a sweat lodge with some special friends. As our small group gathered together, we were instructed to bring large blankets and lay them over the basic structure that had been formed by staking long and flexible tree branches into

---

* Minx Boren, *Soul Notes,* (Palm Beach Gardens, FL: Fourfold Path Inc., 2000): Page 57.

the ground at two-foot intervals in a large circle and then tying them together in the center to form a domed hut. A fire had been burning for hours just outside this primitive structure, and glowing hot coals were now ready to be placed into a pit in the center of the blanketed enclosure. We were invited to enter into this dark, hot, and rather cramped space and settle in for the long night ahead. All this was very new to me. I remember that it felt both odd and sacred to be doing this. There was a leader who told stories, chanted, and beat on a drum.

Over the course of several hours, I drifted in and out of focused attention. Periodically one of the blanket flaps would open and spirits were invited to come and go, along with some of those gathered around the burning coals who chose to not stay longer. Toward the end, there were only a handful of us still in the sweat lodge, and I was lying down on a blanket in a state of peaceful reverie. That is when my mother appeared and sat down beside me. I could see her quite clearly even though she had died many years earlier. She spoke to me gently and asked me to come with her because there was something important that she wanted me to see. I resisted, saying that I was too exhausted to get up, but she explained that only my spirit needed to accompany her. My body could remain where it was.

As I recall my experience in my mind's eye what I remember is that she took my hand and led my spirit-self out of the lodge and into an open field. There was a woman outside, and I recognized her as my grandmother, also long gone from the earth. My mother took her hand, and it was then that I noticed that my grandmother was holding the hand of another woman…and then another…and then another in a vast country field that stretched in front of me as far as my eyes could see. Here we were—all linked together and moving slowly, gracefully, to familiar music in a snakelike and sensual dance that was also familiar to me from my childhood. I asked my mother who these women were, and she explained that they were my lineage stretching back to the beginning of time and that all of them "lived" in me now, that I was the current keeper of the wisdom of all those who had come before me, that it was "my turn" now to live this truth, and to keep it alive and pass it on. After a while, she brought my spirit-self back to join my body and soon after that the sweat lodge experience was over.

But the next phase of my life was only beginning. From that day forward, I felt called to bring women together into sacred conversations—essential dialogues that matter and make a difference. It is a big part of the work I continue to do in the world today.

As I sit here looking for the right words to convey this rather strange yet profound experience, my mind keeps wandering back to other times, places, and people I loved and who loved me—fiercely. I think of my mother whose *mama bear* love tried to protect me from all ills, even when she couldn't protect herself from the disease that caused her so much suffering and claimed her life all too young. I remember so many sweet, small moments together cooking and shopping and doing jigsaw and crossword puzzles. She spent her time, money, and the little energy she had on my joy. She was intelligent, and creative, and she loved life and taught me by example to do the same.

And I remember mama—my mother's mother, who called me *Minxela* and carried me in her capable yet soft arms (I still remember how it felt to be held by her) down the stairs of her apartment and away from a fierce fire when I was a small child. And I remember a hundred visits to that same walk-up apartment on St. John's Place in Brooklyn and how she fussed over me and the sugar cookies we baked together. This simple yet valiant woman, born in Kiev in Russia, raised all her orphan siblings by baking and selling bread and sweets, and was forced, not so many years later and with six children of her own in tow, to flee that home with my grandfather. Somehow, she always kept everyone and everything together…well, almost. One of her daughters was killed by the Cossacks during that time of escape, but my grandmother never succumbed to dismay. There was no time. My own mother was an infant then, being nursed during that whole long and treacherous flight to safety. They made it to America and a new life. And so it is that I am here and that I too have had a chance at life.

Now, as I sit here reminiscing, my sweet Aunt Bea also comes to mind—a matriarch and pillar of strength in her own right. I loved this woman, who became a widow all too young and who raised her two daughters on her own, this woman who then raised her two grandsons when first her son-in-law and then her daughter died way too young, this woman whom I called my second mother because that is who she was for me, this woman who was my mother's eldest sister and truly a mothering presence to her as well, this woman whose strength and love helped me to cope with the challenges of my childhood and beyond.

Warrior women, courageous women, valiant women, determined women, extraordinary ordinary women whose life-songs deserve to be remembered and sung. Perhaps that is why this story has flowed onto this page so easily. This is a small piece of the *herstory* of the lineage from which I come and from which I draw strength and inspiration. They live in me now—are alive in me now—and I am truly blessed. Truth be told, whenever I feel small or not enough or exhausted or am tempted to give up, I remember them and stand up straight and tall, just like they taught me to.

Think about your lineage. *Upon whose shoulders do you stand? Whose legacy and wisdom do you carry within you? How are you bringing forth that which is now yours to share?* As we grow through the decades it is essential that we remember, honor, and celebrate those who have come before, and not just those of our bloodline. There are millions of women over the course of *herstory* who did the right thing, the courageous thing, the necessary thing, so that we could have more opportunities than they had.

Find Your Tribe

and your Bliss Group and your BSSer Buddies
and your Soul Lab Companions

and so here we are
a unique tribe of curious seekers
who have meandered along together
as committed journey mates

loyal to both our own evolution
or, dare I say, transformation
as well as each other's
steadfastly leaning in to one another

We, as humans, are relational by nature and thrive in connection. Indeed, scientists postulate that humans have survived for thousands of years, not because we are the strongest species, but because we learned early on the value of community and cooperation. As George Bernard Shaw remarked, "Independence is middle class blasphemy. We are all dependent, every one of us on earth." Think about it. Just consider what it takes to put food on our tables or to furnish our homes or to build a spaceship to travel to the moon or simply to have available paper clips to tidy up the piles on our desks. No matter the item or the activity, there are thousands upon thousands of interlocking efforts required to make even the most basic things feasible. With the possible exceptions of the Robinson Crusoes of the world, none of us lives on a deserted island forced to fend entirely for ourselves.

Still and all, it is important to remain at choice about where and with whom we establish our strongest roots and connections. To borrow Oprah Winfrey's *"what I know for sure"* phrase, for me it is that we each need to seek out and celebrate those with whom we can be candid, authentic, and free. The quality of our days and the fullness of our lives depend upon the success of this ongoing commitment.

A thread that has woven its way through my life has to do with the importance and value I place on strong relationships. Although I was drawn to create strong individual friendships early on, I did not begin to enjoy the experience of relationships within the context of powerful groups until I was in my mid-twenties. Passionate student that I am, my first groups were found mostly in classroom situations. The conversations were lively, provocative, and insightful but often they were devoid of intimacy and deep introspection. There were also other group involvements through charity work, community projects, and social events. Finally, when I was in my thirties living in New York City, I was invited to join the Bliss Group, which was actually a constellation of dozens of groups composed of ten women in each pod. Within this network were women willing to take responsibility as *the source (or source of bliss)* for what transpired in their own lives and, by extension, in the universe. We were working women, overextended and exhausted in what I would call the age of the *superwoman,* who were determined to be/do/have it all. We were searching for ways to balance our commitments and to learn to express ourselves as powerful and response-able beings. The Bliss network had a profound influence on me. The intimacy of my group and our shared desire to reach beyond our self-imposed limitations created shifts in each and every one of our lives. My Bliss Group provided my first of many *AHAs!* about what it means to thrive in connection.

I was a *Bliss Groupie* (as we called ourselves) for about two years, and during that time my energy became more directed. I took on bigger challenges. I also began taking greater responsibility for what was not working in my life. Mel and I have always been supportive and caring partners. But our marriage was suffering because Mel was experiencing a severe case of Wall Street burnout, and we were stuck in a tumultuous lifestyle that no longer worked for us. Gradually we gained the courage to make a radical change and so, in the fall of 1989, sold our apartment, left our careers, and moved to Florida—a relocation which became the beginning of a totally new chapter of our lives. It was difficult and painful to leave behind a strong network of dear and often longtime friends to start anew. There were many tears, much loneliness, and adjusting. But there has also been a beautiful new home, a new community lifestyle, and many delightful new friends.

Finding my New York City Bliss Group was totally serendipitous. Someone I knew was participating and invited me to join. The next important group showed up just as serendipitously. I had recently moved to Florida and was lecturing at a local health food store. At the end of the presentation, a woman in the audience jumped up to introduce herself and tell me that "we had to get to know each other." This is how I met Susan Klein, who became an instant friend as well as a mentor coach to me. That evening she asked how I liked living in Florida. I replied that, "I would like it a lot better if I could find a women's group." As it turns out, Susan was just starting to create a group, and I was immediately invited to participate. That circle included so many terrific women that I felt I had found "home." We spent many good years gathering each month to delve into soul-searching inquiries together. I also met my first business partner, Cynthia Gracey, in that cluster of women.

By the time that group started winding down, I had gone back to school to become certified as a coach—also because of Susan Klein, a founder of Coach U and the International Coach Federation, as well as one of the first coaches in the world to receive the MCC (Master Certified Coach) designation from the ICF. Susan seems to be my special angel when it comes to serendipitously showing up and pointing the way to what's next. She invited me into a group of local Florida master coaches that was just forming. That was more than twelve years ago, and that group has been gathering monthly by phone, at convenient getaways, and at coach conferences for all these years. We actually call ourselves the BSSers (short for Blue Sky Society, but the acronym is more fun) and consider ourselves a tribe. Defined by Webster's as "a group of persons having a common character, occupation or interest," the BSSers qualify on all three counts. But we have become much more than that for each other. We have been present to and for each other through so many celebrations and challenges that our lives are now totally interwoven and connected.

Then, again rather serendipitously, along came my Soul Lab, another tribe to which I am devoted. In 2005, I studied the basics of the Art of Convening™ with Craig and Patricia Neal and developed a skill set for bringing people together in meaningful dialogue. I went on to do their advanced training and then nine of us students, who wanted to continue to practice and build our proficiency in this modality of coaching, decided to continue gathering together. We have been meeting monthly for more than twelve years, first by teleconference and then via a Zoom platform, choosing a topic of focus for each gathering and taking turns facilitating. We have also been on three retreats together—one in California and two in Minnesota. Together we have dived deeply into some of the most profound and intimate explorations I have ever been privileged to experience. We too have become a tribe by choice and remain committed to our own and each other's growth and well-being.

Real conversation arises when two or more people agree to gather together in the name of a worthy question or quest. Each person offers their wisdom and their thoughtful reflections, adding to the richness of the dialogue. The fascinating thing is that what these encounters yield are not answers, but rather the gift of deeper questions that can have a profound impact. Rabbi Zalman Schachter-Shalomi speaks of "the gentle alchemy of community building." We can each grow through the realizations and insights of others. By wandering alongside, or standing on the shoulders of fellow travelers, we can reach heights of awareness which we might not have access to alone. Because of this, finding those with whom you can grow, experiment, and explore the essential questions of life, those with whom you are willing to allow time and space for the sharing of stories, ideas, and ideals, those who are also on a journey of discovery, is a gift and an important aspect of thriving.

On the other hand, it needs to be mentioned that there are occasions to be wary and cautious. I highly recommend Brené Brown's well researched and brilliantly written book, *Braving the Wilderness: The Quest for True Belonging and the Courage to Stand Alone,* as a guide for anyone seeking to find and experience real community and who wants to avoid the pitfalls of engaging with others when it isn't smart or safe. In my own life, I have at times known the awkwardness and pain of not truly belonging. I have also paid the price for trying to belong in the wrong ways or for the wrong reasons. Ultimately, it is about being present to my own most authentic sense of self *and self-acceptance* that has made all the difference.

Gathering in Community

while the form and formalities of convening
may vary over time and
because of the human vessels
that embrace it and carry it forward
the foundation of good practices
and good intentions will remain
as long as there are those of us who remember
always to speak from our hearts
without preconceived notions or ideologies
and to create opportunities
for others to do the same

In this tweeting, texting world, I find myself wondering whether the art of real and connective conversation will be lost like other great human skills that have become obsolete, such as navigating by starlight or starting a fire using only dried sticks or tending to a vegetable garden in our own backyard.

To find ways to counteract this trend, I have spent years training in and practicing the Art of Convening™ as I have mentioned before. This is a process developed by Craig and Patricia Neal and expanded upon in their book by the same name. It outlines in detail a particular way of gathering together in community that allows our individual and collective wisdom to emerge in the spaciousness of a time and place that is purposefully created by certain procedures and rituals. These groups may be made up of like-minded or diverse participants, friends or strangers, colleagues or competitors. They often span many other differences as well, including age, sex, culture, interests, and expertise. For me, the great *AHA!* was witnessing a method that offered a surer path to deep and meaningful connection. What creates a cohesive whole is, first and foremost, the intention to develop this sense of unity, and, secondly, a series of specific rituals and practices designed to establish a container of safety and acceptance that allows all voices to be respectfully heard. The result is both magical and moving as well as practical and powerful.

Here is one simple practice based on a process used in the Art of Convening™: First, offer a sincere invitation to those you would like to join you in a circle gathering. Once you are all together, sit in a circle and place a lit candle in the center to evoke the image of a campfire as a reminder of the way our ancestors gathered since time immemorial. To ensure the full engagement of each participant, take time to invite each person's support and wisdom through a ritual that is sometimes referred to as *stringing the beads*. In this ceremony, you ask each participant to imagine that every person present is a unique and precious bead, and your voices are the string that will link you together into one beautiful necklace. This process, which is based on many ancient traditions that respect the value of deep listening and heartfelt speaking, allows every voice to be heard.

Now ask an inviting question like, *"What's alive in you right now?"* Allow each participant to take a turn speaking without interruption. If you need to limit the amount of time each person speaks due to time constraints, use a timer and gently ring a bell or chime as a reminder when their time allotment is coming to an end. Instruct them to say, "I have spoken" or "these are my words" as a way to ensure that they have been allowed to fully express their thoughts. The listeners respond with "Thank you" or "I have heard your words." When all the voices have been heard, open up the circle for further conversation and expansion on the thoughts expressed.

Margaret Wheatley, one of my favorite thought leaders, wrote a book titled *Turning to One Another: Simple Conversations to Restore Hope to the Future*. As the title so eloquently suggests, our best hope for the future lies in our ability to turn to one another with curiosity and respect. *With whom might you be drawn to do this now?*

Surrender Before You Have To

"May I meet this moment fully.
May I see it as a friend."

~BUDDHIST PRAYER, SPOKEN BY AUTHOR AND
MINDFULNESS TEACHER SYLVIA BOORSTEIN AT
SPIRIT ROCK ONE EVENING AS I SAT AT HER FEET—
AS MAGNIFICENT AN *AHA! MOMENT* AS
I HAVE EVER EXPERIENCED

*D*o *you ever feel bogged down, inert, immobilized beyond rhyme or reason?* I don't know about you, but I get stuck sometimes. Actually, more than sometimes. When I have gotten myself wedged into that stuck place, it can feel as if I am never going to find the wherewithal to budge. Sometimes all the self-cheerleading in the world isn't effective. I go through pep talks *("You are bigger and stronger than this challenge.")* and affirmations *("I am a resilient and capable woman.")* and, I confess, sometimes even *less-than-loving* self-babble *("Who do you think you are to just give up? Anyone with half a mind could get this handled. What's wrong with you?")*. Of course, there are times when neither my inner bantering nor verbal battering work.

Have you ever noticed how we, as humans, want so much to be in control that we sometimes desperately try to cling to a certain sense of orderliness in our lives, no matter the truth of the circumstances? Have you ever found yourself stuck in a certain way of seeing things that has left you sad and disheartened, no matter your attempts to think your way clear?

Here is what I have noticed. Mostly, it is about surrender. When I am done wallowing or railing at myself or the gods or fate or the horrible state of the world, and simply let go, things finally begin to shift. Almost imperceptibly at first, a glimmer of an idea or a possibility will peek out from the gloom. Other times, the first pull out of the muck comes from the hand of a friend who is willing to quietly and lovingly be there for me without judgment, agenda, or advice. Then, too, there are magical moments when a "message" arrives via a book or a conversation or even something as far-fetched as a TV advertisement. It doesn't matter how or when or where the nudge comes from, I am always grateful for its appearance.

In the times of not knowing, of not being sure, the question is *how can you wait patiently in the twist of your tangled mind and heart for whatever it is that will loosen the constraints that bind you and show you the next best way to turn?* Would that I could just wait patiently, but instead I notice how often my confusion and uncertainty surface. Yet I also know that when, in my impatient foolishness, I have forced myself to be decisive and to choose, these premature knee jerk reactions have left me unsatisfied and, at times, at risk.

Iyanla Vanzant, author, inspirational speaker and TV personality, invites her listeners to "stay open. There is something bigger than you know going on here." Something bigger may be percolating up from whatever depths of insecurity and not knowing I may have plummeted into. When I can remain open while confronted with my lack of surety, the process becomes one of unfolding into something spacious rather than unraveling into chaos. Of course, in the midst of the most dramatic and challenging moments, this is easier said than done. It requires both my will and my willingness—the will to not allow myself to wallow in despair or spiral down into helplessness and the willingness to use every inner and outer resource at my disposal to stay accepting and receptive.

I have also come to understand that to get unstuck, my gaze has to shift to something bigger. I have to be willing to see the whole and wholeness of what is true at this time of my life. Then I can see the unfolding of a potentially larger story. When I am able to broaden my outlook, I can at last find the clarity and courage to pick myself up, dust myself off, and move beyond my critical self-talk and self-imposed limitations to a wider, more accepting sense of self and circumstance. I am reminded of how I need to constantly re-accommodate to LIFE.

One of the most marvelous trainings I ever went through was to become a facilitator of the Transformation Game®, a life and learning experience played on a game-board, complete with opportunity squares, setback squares, appreciation squares, miracle squares, angel squares, and more. It is still one of my favorite ways to coach clients through a difficult time, and to invite them to think way outside the box for possible next steps and opportunities. I mention the game here because, in order to complete the training, a group of us spent ten days in North Carolina with Joy Drake and Kathy Tyler, the creators of this unique game, playing it over and over and over again, choosing a different "issue" or "challenge" for each go round. What was especially fascinating and telling for me was that the angel of "Surrender" showed up more than once. I didn't understand why. I am a rather disciplined and determined woman, and I know how to find the grit and gumption to do what needs to be done. Then came the *AHA!* because what I didn't know how to do was surrender, let go, and allow something beyond my unwavering doggedness to reveal a gentler way. Learning to surrender is, for me, an ongoing challenge. I keep that angel card on my desk atop a crystal in front of my computer screen as an everyday reminder to be gentler with myself and more at ease with the way life unfolds.

I have heard Angeles Arrien, Joan Borysenko, and other spiritual leaders speak about the four rules of life and how important it is to: 1) Show up. 2) Pay attention (to what has heart and meaning). 3) Tell the truth (without blame or judgment). 4) Don't be attached to the outcome. As I've matured, I've gotten better at the first three. It's the last rule that is so very tough. Equanimity is not my strong suit. I have all sorts of opinions about how things could and should turn out. It is not only very difficult, but also rather humbling to let go, give up control, and just be with what is in any given moment. But, as I am learning, it is also less exhausting. When I stop struggling and take a breath, the gift I receive is ease and the lesson I learn is to trust.

In the practice of yoga, we are instructed to "receive a breath" rather than "take a breath." What a magnificent reminder to go easy rather than gasp and grasp at things. Years ago, after going through bilateral total hip replacements, I found myself unable to walk without intense pain in one leg at the point where the prosthesis ended mid-femur. After a year of therapy, which did not measurably alleviate the severe discomfort, I decided that I needed to "reclaim" my life and accept what was. I took myself away to Santa Fe to a prayer retreat led by Wayne Muller, a minister and the author of several books that have inspired me, including *How Then Shall We Live? Four Simple Questions that Reveal the Beauty and Meaning of Our Lives* (talk about inspiring questions!!!) and *Learning to Pray: How We Find Heaven on Earth.* I spent five days chanting, weaving, whispering, drumming, writing down, and drawing my prayers. And I breathed a lot. Slowly and deeply and self-lovingly. Day by day I let go of the struggle and came to terms with how things were. Nothing miraculous happened at the retreat, but somehow I still left feeling more at peace.

I also came away from that experience with the simple prayer, "Thy will be done. Show me." And truly, I was shown. First, the next right opportunity in my career knocked at my door, and I began offering workshops titled "Extraordinary Self-Care in Times of Crisis" because that was exactly what I was learning about. Then, because of a compassionate friend, I was gifted with a session with a physical therapist who determined the cause of the pain as well as the steps to take to teach my body to find a new equilibrium and to heal. A few weeks later, I was pain-free and have remained so ever since.

Which brings me to the whole conversation about miracles and the whole realm of what we don't even know we don't know. Think of life as a pie with three wedges. The first very slim wedge is what we know (or at least think we know). The second somewhat larger slice of the pie is what we know we don't know (everything from how to win the lottery to quantum physics to how to fly a plane and so much more). Then there is this great big piece of the pie that represents the whole realm of what we don't even know we don't know. We can think and strategize and plan and guesstimate but, more often than not, the great opportunities and blessings in our lives arrive from the ethers of the unknown.

If Einstein is correct, then "anyone who doesn't believe in miracles isn't a realist." So perhaps if we are willing to surrender, and yet also stay open to that which is beyond our current reality or ability to understand, we can find the peacefulness to "meet this moment fully [and] see it as a friend." It is a practice worth pursuing.

Give It Up

beyond the exhaustion of
endless striving and perpetual
walls to scale and information to devour
there is this other way entirely
available to the extent
that I can muster up the courage
to loosen the yoke of insufficiency
to which I have for so long
hitched myself

A sequel to the whole idea of surrender is to give up on managing the onslaught of information with which we are bombarded day in and day out. Admit it. No matter your great intentions or your willingness to burn the candle at both ends, you are never going to catch up. Yet, if by some miracle, you do catch up for a minute and a half, you are never going to keep up. It's time to call a truce and liberate yourself from the endless piles of magazines or the countless emails you are never going to get to (even though you KNOW that their contents would vastly improve your life IF you could implement even just some of the good suggestions proffered). The barrage of useful, good, interesting, and perhaps even vital information, is endless and ubiquitous.

Since I am a firm believer in walking my talk, I just took a break from writing this to carry eight shopping bags of magazines to the recycle bin. AND I just deleted 3,800 probably impressively informative emails with all sorts of terrific tips about health and fixing things and how to achieve the perfect yoga pose and great bargains and thoughts on saving the planet and links to even more inspirational stuff. But, you might argue, emails are in cyberspace and don't really take up physical space the way the magazines piled high in my bathroom do (the only corner I could find for them). Yet because every time I open my email box, there they are—all 3,800 (and growing) of them glaring at me, waiting for me to do something. I become exhausted and defeated by the prospect of tackling them one by one.

AHA! I give up. I surrender to the absolute certainty that I will never know enough…or at least never know about all that I wish I could. No, I am not a defeatist, but, considering that there are new ideas being generated every single day, what hope can there be for ever navigating all this? It really is all too much. We are never going to know it all (and do we really want to become a *know it all?*). So be it.

So, what's a person to do? CHOOSE! I know it's tough, but if you can resign yourself to eensy teensy victories—say one or two good articles in a magazine or two of your choosing. That way at least you are staying engaged. Lately, I am enjoying Oprah's ever mindful and encouraging publication as well as *Spiritual Health.* Add to these one or two inspirational eNewsletters (I opt for *The Optimist* and *Upworthiest* because they lift my spirits and give me hope). Then there is *Take the Lead Women*, which I read because I am passionate about building strong female leaders and am an advocate for gender equity in the workplace. I suppose I should mention that I also follow the *Food Babe* whose emails keep me abreast of what is going on about improving the quality of our food supply.

The next thing to consider is, *do you really need (or even want) to read the newspaper from cover to cover every day?* It's so depressing. Find ways to limit your daily dose of trauma and drama. It can't be healthy to ingest so much negativity each day. Maybe even do something radically breath-giving instead like taking a month-long break from the news and going for daily walks in the time you have freed up.

Another great idea is to buddy up. Divvy up the best of the best things being written with some friends and then share what you discover. If you can each learn one tiny interesting thing each day THAT might be enough.

Right now, I am feeling like a true revolutionary. Perhaps I should carry a placard—*"Down with Endless Information. Up with Naps and Quiet Hours. Down with depressing predictions. Up with intuitive forays into our own uplifting inklings and knowings." Care to join me? What would you like your placard to say? And what corner of your home or office or computer are you now willing to tackle in order to make some space in your life?*

PART TWO

AHA! MOMENTS— GROWING ONGOINGLY

"All my life I used to wonder what I would become when I grew up. Then, about seven years ago, I realized that I was never going to grow up—that growing is an ever ongoing process."
~M. SCOTT PECK, AMERICAN PSYCHIATRIST AND AUTHOR

Resilience Matters

"When medieval monks were asked how they practiced their faith, they would often reply, 'By falling down and getting up.' And there you have the whole muddled mess of being human."

~MARK NEPO, AMERICAN AUTHOR, PHILOSOPHER, POET, TEACHER

Resilience is admirable, stirring, stunning, oftentimes audacious, and always awesome. I appreciate resilience. Actually, it blows me away. For example, as I wrote in a previous book about healing, "There is something about being human and yet rising above human predicaments that is inspiring. It is how we create and achieve even beyond our wildest imaginings and in the face of incalculable obstacles. So many of my heroes and heroines are those who make of their lives something significant and authentic, worthy of their time and energy and in spite of all that would wear them down or block their way."*

I first met Mark Nepo at a prayer retreat in Santa Fe, New Mexico. The retreat was being facilitated by Wayne Muller, author of *How Then Shall We Live Knowing We Shall Die*, a book that so resonated with me to the very core of my being that I wanted to attend and learn more. Muller is both a minister and a psychologist, as well as the founder of Bread for the Journey. This charitable organization does a worthy job of focusing on the plight of the very poor through the development of compassionate programs that rely on small communities of local

---

* Minx Boren, *Healing is a Journey: find your own path to hope, recovery, and wellness* (Boulder, CO: Blue Mountain Arts, 2014): Page 29.

volunteers. These helpers identify a need and then provide considerable hands-on *sweat equity*, relying on only small donations to fund projects.

Mark was at the retreat as the poet-in-residence, as well as to share the moving story of his own healing from brain cancer. I was there because I was facing my own physical challenge. I had run out of traditional options for finding relief, and I was seeking the comfort and inspiration of prayer. All forty-something participants at all ages and stages of life were there with open hearts and minds to come to terms with whatever they were coping with and to tap into their own resilience while finding greater meaning in their lives. As I sat together with these beautiful beings, listening to their stories day after day, I experienced *AHA! moment after moment.* Their resilience touched me deeply. Their ability to show up again and again with grit and gumption, with grace and gusto, no matter the obstacles and challenges that may conspire against them, inspired me. I recognized within each of them a very human and superhuman capacity to choose to not give up, but rather to face the future with clarity and courage no matter the current conditions. The stories told were about having the strength and wherewithal to bounce back and to even find ways to thrive after setbacks, failures, disappointments, and losses. As I witnessed their magnificent spirits, I sensed my own resilience being rekindled.

Are there stories of resilience that inspire you and sometimes give you the strength to carry on? There are so many extraordinary people who leave us awed by their capacity to not only survive and endure but to thrive and create in the throes of difficult circumstances. Christopher Reeve's paralysis, Helen Keller's blindness, and Beethoven's deafness have become archetypal stories of accepting and then surmounting physical challenges. But there are also countless ordinary people who suffer illness or loss or abandonment or defeat, and ultimately move past their anger, frustration, and grief. In so doing, they demonstrate a quality of resilience that touches our hearts. Even the ordinary act of growing older with grace and dignity becomes inspirational when viewed through a certain lens.

There are times when life is laid back and easy, when we can simply savor our moments and the blessings that fill our days are easy to count. Then there are times when life throws a hard punch to the gut and we are—at least momentarily—down for the count, wind and will knocked out of us. The question is: *What is it that you draw upon deep within you to rise to whatever occasion or challenge life sends your way?* Whether it's a financial, physical, or personal crisis, there lives within us an inner resourcefulness available if we are willing to seek it out. And, all around us, there are outer resources that we can tap into to support us along the way.

Yet what I notice in my own life, and in the lives of others, is that the first crucial step toward moving beyond setbacks and limitations is the simple acceptance of what is so. To live fully, we need to acknowledge all circumstances—ease and uncertainty, happiness and sadness, and vital well-being as well as pain. In his book, *The Beethoven Factor*, Dr. Paul Pearsall marvels at how Beethoven wrote and conducted his Ode to Joy *after* he went deaf. Pearsall reflects on what it is that allows us to thrive even in the midst of such adversity. He defines *thriving* as "reconstructing life's meaning in response to life's most destructive occurrences." Pearsall contrasts it to the antithetical state of emotional and spiritual fatigue he refers to as *"languishing."*

In what ways do you consider yourself resilient? How effectively do YOU manage the muddled messiness of being human? We don't need to wait until times of crisis force us into action. We can learn to really thrive—rather than just survive—by continually cultivating optimism, positive energy, trust, hope, and sense of connection. It's not just about rebounding in times of crisis. As Pearsall says, it's about "conducting our daily life as an ode to joy."

In order to become a *"thriver,"* we must step out of the frenzy of reactive "doing" long enough to be still and listen for that wise inner voice. Only then can we tap into our capacity to become appropriately responsive. Ask yourself: *Which practices awaken my resilience and fortify my hopefulness? Who are the people who support and encourage me? Where are the places that heal and recharge me? What are the possibilities, alternatives, and choices that are available to me now?* You might want to keep a journal to both capture and carefully consider your reflections. You'll know you are on the right track when you experience a sense of relief, perhaps even excitement, when you're filled up by what you decide to do rather than feeling drained.

I recently saw a documentary on the life of Frida Kahlo, the Mexican artist who started painting seriously after she became bedridden from an accident. She painted her pain, hopes, fears, nightmares, passions, angers, and disgust with great power and skill. She laid herself bare on the canvas. In spite of persistent and excruciating pain and a tempestuous marriage, she led an impressively productive life, leaving a legacy of some of the most riveting art I have ever seen. She could so easily have curled up in a corner and suffered away her days. That she did not is in itself astonishing. I stand in awe of her resilience and wonder, *in what small ways can I learn to astonish myself each day?*

Building Your Resilience Muscle

Here are some ways to develop and bolster resilience:

1. Get real. Recognize setbacks and disappointments for what they are. At the same time don't catastrophize. Every loss is not a deal breaker.

2. Learn from your experiences. Even if you "lose," don't lose the lesson.

3. In the tough times, pay attention to your true feelings—name them and talk or write about them—and then do whatever it takes to shift to a more positive way of being. Often this requires finding meaning and purpose in and through your circumstances.

4. When the stress hits the fan, find ways to think creatively and flexibly about whatever is going on. Resilience is built one expansive response at a time.

5. The old adage, "When the going gets tough, the tough get going," holds true. Don't just curl up or cave in. Find the thing you can do, a next step you can take, no matter how small or seemingly insignificant.

6. Don't go it alone. Recognize and acknowledge those who have your back and your best interests at heart. Call on them. Lean on them. Brainstorm with them. Two (or three or five) heads are truly better than one.

7. Take great care, especially when the pressure is on or plans fall apart. Rather than sacrificing sleep or exercise or good food choices in order to relentlessly keep your nose to the grindstone, remember to take a

break. Actually, take lots of them. Get enough rest. Get revitalized. Get out in nature to clear your head. In the long run, you will reap the benefits of this thoughtful self-care.

Forgiveness Matters

how strong
my reluctance
to relinquish endless
inner lists of failure
and inadequacies...

how compelling
my longing
to experience at last
the simplicity
*of unencumbered being**

Have you ever experienced the ways and times books can become teach-ers? Ever since I was a young girl I have been drawn to read-ing across a wide spectrum of themes and topics and have been richly rewarded by the many books that have touched my life. Somehow the right volume always seems to appear in front of me with the perfect message at the perfect time, whether it falls off a shelf at my feet or is handed to me by a friend or is mentioned to me by so many people that I realize I am supposed to be paying attention. When I read, I always underline and scribble comments, questions, thoughts, arguments, con-cerns, and opinions in the margins. In that way I feel as if I am actively

---

* An original shorter version of this chapter along with the poem *how strong my reluctance* first appeared in Minx Boren, *Healing Is a Journey—Finding your own path to hope, recov-ery, and wellness* (Boulder, CO: Blue Mountain Arts, 2014): Pages 36–38.

participating in a dialogue with the author. This technique has served me well.

Years ago, I read Robin Casarjian's *Forgiveness—A Bold Choice for a Peaceful Heart*. The book proved to be transformational and inspired me with a whole string of *AHA! moments*. As I came to recognize all the ways I held on to grievances and old stories, I also realized what the cost was to myself, beyond the impact to those I would not forgive. Carrying around so much anger and sadness robbed me of joy, energy, and power. To add to the burden, I have become sensitive in these elder years to the fact that, with each passing decade, there tend to accumulate more and more opportunities to be angry and unforgiving. The longer we live, the more upsetting things there are to which we become witness.

As the experts point out, often our anger is self-directed. I don't know about you, but I most certainly have this little inner critic who sits on my shoulder whispering nasty nothings in my ear about all the ways I am or do less than I believe I should. Yet, as the Buddha said, "You, yourself, as much as anybody in the entire universe, deserve your love and affection." And, I would add, forgiveness.

The Museum of Tolerance, located in Los Angeles, has two entrances—one for tolerant people and the other for everyone else. If you try to open the door reserved for the tolerant you will find that it is locked. Why? Because, of course, none of us is without predispositions or judgments. Therein lies a key to forgiveness. We each have opinions and prejudices about just about everything and it is only when we can recognize and forgive our own biases that we can begin to make the shift to non-reactive acceptance and forgiveness of others.

What the years have taught me is that there are two sides to forgiveness. The first person I must bless with forgiveness is always myself. Only then can I expand my open-heartedness to another. Only then can I walk in the shoes of another and attempt to understand what prompted their words and/or actions. Only then can I embrace my and their brokenness as integral to our humanity.

Have you ever experienced how those you know best can sometimes astound you by offering a level of awareness that was previously unavailable? Early one morning, while still in bed, my husband turned to me and said, "I'm sorry." I was puzzled because I couldn't imagine why. So I asked, "For what?" and he replied, "I don't know. I just thought that, in case I mess up somehow today, I want you to know that I'm sorry." Then he smiled his brilliantly playful smile before we both got up and were swept up into the busyness of the day. But I kept thinking about his words. On the one hand, isn't it true that, if we inadvertently do something that isn't quite right or disappoint someone somehow, we want to be forgiven, want it to be known that it wasn't on purpose? Yet, on the other hand, I kept wondering if I had become so "critical" or had expressed disappointment one time too many. Had I left him feeling confused and vulnerable as to what he believed I expected of him? His words that morning sparked an *AHA! moment.* Something shifted and we both became more playful and lighthearted about the inevitable ways we as humans (and as a couple) inevitably bump up against each other from time to time. Perhaps there is something within us, beneath the surface of our transgressions and imperfections, which simply wants to be understood, to be loved unconditionally, so that we can count on being given a "pass" or "get out of jail free" card should we need one.

Another forgiveness dilemma shows up when, no matter how hard we try, it's never quite good enough. There have been times when I have stayed in a relationship where it felt as if I were walking on eggshells. No matter what I said or didn't say, did or didn't do, sooner or later I crossed some vague line in the sand and did something that was perceived as "wrong" or disappointing. To find my way through these circumstances, I had to both forgive myself in advance for not doing the right thing *and* also recognize that sometimes when someone feels offended it may have absolutely nothing to do with me.

Perhaps you have experienced these things as well. I urge you to seek out the rich and rewarding paths to forgiving yourself and all those whose lives touch yours.

Stop. LISTEN. Wait.

"It seems rather incongruous that in a society of super sophisticated communication, we often suffer from a shortage of listeners."

~ERMA BOMBECK, HUMORIST, COLUMNIST, AUTHOR

"**W**hy are you speaking?" Those are the words prominently displayed on a sign that sits on my desk. It's an ongoing reminder that I learn much more by keeping my mouth shut and paying attention than I do by talking. As a coach, I am trained to ask compelling questions. I know I've done my job well when a client says, "Hmmmm. What an interesting question. Let me think about that." Bingo. That's means I am on track and then what is mine to do is to simply stop and grant them the spaciousness to work through their response. Then I need to listen…and LISTEN…and **LISTEN** some more while they consider and shape thoughts into language. I need to wait until I am sure they have exhausted their own mulling process. If need be, I might spice it up a bit by asking "And what else?"…and then asking it again…and again! Another truly terrific coach question, when someone responds to something you have asked by saying "I don't know" is to ask, "What if you did know?" That gets their attention and gets them to dig deeper in order to discover some more profound level of knowing. Interestingly, something essential usually surfaces as a result of these inquiries.

AHA! Coaching has taught me that good listening is "an advanced art form." So said Thomas Leonard, founder of Coach U. "It is one thing to listen to a person attentively. This is nice and it's polite. However, the art of actually hearing someone, understanding what they are saying, what they mean, what that means, and then responding to that [requires] plenty of wisdom, compassion, strength and encouragement…" I have heard of a study of medical doctors which showed that they spend an average of thirty seconds listening to their patients' concerns before interrupting and directing the conversation. When asked to remain quiet until their patients completed their list of concerns, it took only three and a half minutes for patients to feel listened to *and* the doctor found out more than he could have by following his own agenda of questions. Imagine that. Here's another inspirational story. Dr. John Nigerian, the surgeon who performed the first liver transplant in the 1970s, wheels every one of his patients to their car when discharged so that he can connect with them one last time. What a powerful way for someone to feel seen and known at such a vulnerable time in life. As Mark Twain quipped, "What most people really need is a good listening to."

Beyond the immediate answers given, when listening deeply it is vital to listen beyond the words for what is not being said, for what is truly most important (often it is not what people say it is), for what is needed right now in the moment, for what is lacking or in the way, for false premises and assumptions, and for a whole lot more. We are complex beings and there's always a lot going on beneath the surface of conversations. I have trained in Conversational Intelligence—C-IQ®— with Judith Glaser, and I particularly love the concept of "double-clicking" on words. What someone says, what they mean, what we hear, and how we interpret what they are saying can all leave us on shaky ground. Yet clarity and precision matter if we are going to truly understand one another. This skill goes way beyond coaching. As compassionate human beings, what is ours to do is to attend to what someone is attempting to say and to help them to say it by listening well and by asking clarifying questions when necessary. A simple example would be when someone says, "I wish I/you were more…*fill in the blank (attentive, courageous, willing, kind, focused, playful, etc.)*" The double-click question would be: 'What would THAT look like?'

Another essential aspect of listening has to do with quieting our own inner chatter. We cannot really hear one another if we are listening with our answers running in the background or our ongoing opinions, assumptions, and beliefs playing havoc with our ability to open our hearts as well as our minds to the person in front of us. Another common default listening habit is the *"happy hooker,"* so named by Adele Lynn in *The EI Activity Book.* This behavior shows up when we only listen long enough to "hook" or steer the conversation where we want it to go.

Poor listening skills may develop because many of us suffer from what communicator Nido Qubein terms "agenda anxiety"—the feeling that what we want to say to others is more important than what they might want to say to us. Sometimes we try to impress rather than express, not realizing that two monologues do not constitute a dialogue. Ultimately, in order to dive deeply into a truly connective conversation, we must be willing to be changed by what we hear—again and again. That's not easy because we also want to hold tightly to our beliefs, stay in control, and not be confused or challenged by new facts. But here's the thing, as Theodore Roosevelt knew, "No one cares how much you know until they know how much you care." To add to this thought and take it to the next level, when we listen to someone with genuine interest and without filters or judgments, we often *lean* in their direction, like a flower toward the sun.

I am reminded of a story about a coach colleague and myself. Lable and I were seated together at an event for coaches, and I remember feeling rather ignored the whole evening. I simply made the assumption that he didn't find me particularly interesting and preferred his companion seated on the other side of him. The following year I was once again seated next to him and this time we had a terrific exchange that lasted all evening. Rather than stew about what had happened the previous year, at the end of our time together, I asked him why he had totally ignored me. Turns out that at that dinner I had been seated on the side of his deaf ear!!! He simply didn't hear a word I had said and didn't bother to tell me. YIKES. So much for my assumptions and judgments. We both had a good laugh over it, *and* I learned something important about engagement and how to really request someone's attention (hints: don't be shy about it and don't assume it's about you).

I believe in the power of stories. I believe that poet and political activist Muriel Rukeyser was right when she said, "The world is made up of stories, not atoms." Having spent years training in the Art of Convening™, I can attest to the importance of gathering in community and creating a spaciousness of time and quietude where all the voices can be heard. As we share our stories, we begin to see the fuller fabric of our community, both what we have in common as well as our differences.

My longtime friend and fellow convener Paul Strickland puts it this way; "Telling our stories enables us to rediscover or reclaim our own wholeness. We find that our lives, with all their wonders and their pains, are merely a string of incidents until we write the stories in our own minds and speak them from our own hearts. This hunger for stories is part of what makes us human. Most people grasp immediately that telling their own stories does matter, that these stories need to be told and heard, and that, in their giving and receiving, the possibility of healing is born." *Is there a story you are yearning to share?*

Flourish

*"Life will bring you pain all by itself.
Your responsibility is to create joy."*
~MILTON ERICKSON, M.D.
AMERICAN PSYCHIATRIST AND PSYCHOLOGIST

At some point in time, if we are wise, we mature enough to take responsibility for our life—the whole of it—both good and less than positive choices alike. We recognize and appreciate all that we have done and not done to bring us to this point in time. Yet, at every age, there is still time to influence how much joy, satisfaction, and well-being we are able to experience and embrace.

What is happiness anyway? It was deemed an important enough concept for our founding fathers to actually guarantee our right to pursue it. Research has shown that happiness is our most creative, productive, and responsive state. Happy people are hardier, healthier, and more optimistic. They are therefore more willing to do whatever is necessary to take positive steps toward a satisfying and meaningful future. In business, happiness has actually been shown to impact the bottom line because it opens us up to new possibilities, ideas, and collaborative relationships while energizing us to both take action and follow through.

My own *AHA!* about this thing called happiness occurred just a few years after I decided to go through the Coach U program and the International Coach Federation certification procedure to become a credentialed coach. Diving into the whole field of coaching proved to be a richly rewarding pursuit and one of the best things I've ever done. Every class and every conversation were worthwhile and provocative. Then, as luck would have it, after graduating, I enrolled in the first-ever program on Authentic Happiness Coaching created and led by Dr. Martin Seligman, the author of three ground-breaking books—*Learned Optimism, Authentic Happiness*, and *Flourish*, along with several of his colleagues who were exploring and doing research in this brand-new field. They were all brilliant, focused, and inspiring.

Being exposed to the whole concept of Authentic Happiness changed both my worldview and my focus. I have always been considered an optimist, and perhaps even a Pollyanna. I am always looking for the bright side. Here at last was a perspective that allows people to consider or reconsider their lives from the vantage point of what makes them come alive and thrive, even in the most difficult of times. Here at last were proven tools that could increase their happiness quotient and move them beyond a negative mindset to a more life-enhancing way of seeing and being. I was hooked. Upon completing the AHC program in 2005, this approach became the cornerstone of my coaching philosophy. I feel blessed to have been introduced to this uplifting and life-changing perspective for my own sake and for the sake of what I have been able to offer my clients over these many years.

What does it mean to flourish? Over time the teachings of that first Authentic Happiness course have expanded beyond the idea of happiness to incorporate the broader concepts of well-being and what it means to live a fulfilling life—to flourish. I love the word *flourish* and what it evokes—a sense of thriving, growing luxuriantly, and bursting forth boldly and unabashedly. The root *flor* is connected to the concept of flowering. Those who flourish are those who blossom and come fully into their own, brandishing a certain flush of self-sufficiency and flair for life.

In the relatively new field of positive psychology, Dr. Seligman has been one of those at the helm of an exploration focused on ways to increase our capacity for happiness and true satisfaction. He and other researchers have identified and expanded upon certain behaviors that those who truly flourish have in common. They do each of the following for its own sake, with no outside or further motivation:

They focus on *positive emotions*—cultivating good feelings and allowing themselves to enjoy whatever they are doing.

1. They make time for full *engagement* and rapt attention by eliminating distractions and interruptions and becoming deeply immersed in significant and satisfying tasks. One of the ways they do this is by taking time for *pleasure,* for savoring the moment.

2. They cultivate and honor *positive relationships* and participate with others. We as human are social animals and thrive in connection. In positive psychology there are twenty-four "*signature strengths.*" The strength of *relationship* is defined as "the capacity to love and be loved."

3. They create *meaning* and a sense of *purpose* by focusing on more than just themselves and doing things they deem important, worthwhile, and in service to their friends, their communities, and the world.

4. They enjoy and celebrate *accomplishments*, big and small, that provide a special sense of satisfaction—pursuing success, winning, achievement, and mastery for their own sake.

Okay. So, there you have the *very* brief summary notes. A useful summary acronym for all this is PERMA—Positive Emotions, Engagement (and pleasureful practices), Positive Relationships, Meaning, and Accomplishment. When we are truly involved with life, our days seem to roll merrily along, and we rarely pay much attention to just how content we are in any given moment or why. Thoughts about happiness and satisfaction are more likely to rise to the surface when we are *less than* happy and satisfied, because that's when we recognize that something is missing. That's when we start to wonder about what needs to be done to bring back our joy and spark our enthusiasm. That's when we take stock of what's going on and attempt to determine who or what might be robbing us of our happiness and (if we are wise) how much we might be sabotaging it ourselves. That's when the science of positive psychology becomes a key to getting back and staying on track.

I live by the mantra that "knowing isn't doing." So, when I hear something that inspires me, I look for ways to incorporate it into my life, at least for a while as an experiment to decide if it works for me. This does! I have actually taken this concept of *flourishing* to heart and spend time just before bed each evening journaling about specific ways my life has felt fulfilling that day. I ask myself these questions:

Daily Review Questions: *What positive emotions and pleasures did I enjoy? When did I allow myself to become thoroughly engaged and immersed in some project or pursuit that captivated my time and focus? With whom did I connect deeply? What about today's activities felt meaningful and purposeful? What activity gave me the greatest sense of accomplishment?*

This ritual brings an added measure of pleasure to my day, no matter how deep I have to dig at times in order to find the flourishing moments in the midst of the messiness of how life actually unfolds. They are almost always there, and when they are not, that too serves as a reminder of how I need to allow myself to embrace tomorrow's possibilities. By the way, my journaling process is a variation of *Three Blessings* or *Three Good Things*, where one writes down three of the most special moments of the day. This is one of the most effective exercises in the positive psychology tool kit. I urge you to try it.

Beyond the daily review questions, *other questions worth asking yourself are: In what ways am I taking responsibility for creating my most fulfilling life? What commitments, practices, attitudes, and outlooks am I choosing to embrace in my very own pursuit of happiness? What is one thing I am willing to commit to right now that could expand my capacity for living a flourishing life? BY WHEN (always an essential coach question) will I take action?*

Creativity Matters

"To live a creative life, we must lose our fear of being wrong."
~JOSEPH CHILTON PEARCE, AMERICAN AUTHOR

...and, I would add, our fear of not being perfect!

Okay, I confess. I honestly don't consider myself an artist. I certainly have no ability to draw or paint. Yet, years ago, at an art class taught by a dear friend of mine, Patti Burris, whose paintings have graced the covers of four of my books, I found these rather pleasing colorful "expressions" showing up on the paper, thanks to Patti's excellent instructions and her invitation to simply be playful with absolutely no judgments. What a delightful *AHA! moment.* Somehow, miraculously, I was absolutely tickled by what found its way onto the canvas. I actually kept my "creations" from that one class for years and, eventually, incorporated them into my CoachMinx.com website.

Here's another confession. While I am a poet who has published four books of poetry and two more books that incorporate poems, and have had my poems included in various anthologies, I am still amazed by the process that allows the words to flow onto the page. I often feel as if the poems are gifted to me by the Universe, by something much greater and grander than myself. So it is that, when I am willing to sit quietly and invite these creations to take shape, I am both grateful and humbled by what shows up. It is difficult to explain how surprised and delighted I am by the words that tumble onto the page because while, of course, they are my writings from my very own pen, there is something about them that feels way beyond what I would "produce" just by working diligently at getting them down. It is a very different method from the one I use to write essays like this one, which are more linearly organized. Yet even these writings usually produce unexpected observations that go beyond my early outlines.

Clients sometimes ask me about how to become creative. Actually, the truth is we cannot NOT be. Life is a creative process and we are part of that living energy. Every thought, word, action is a reflection of a creative force that is our birthright. The more important question is how to harness that energy to create something worthwhile? Whether it be a piece of art or a musical composition or a delicious meal or a well-designed business project, the basics of creativity are in our bones. What is ours to do is to move forward with intention and attention. Setting an intention to create something/anything while letting go of preconceived notions of exactly how it must turn out is the first step. Then simply paying attention to inner inklings and *knowings* that appear along the way is the best way to tap into new possibilities. Innovation is all about exploring, experimenting, contemplating, inventing, taking risks, making mistakes, being playful and, above all, enjoying the process. Allow your heart and mind to imagine and dream. Then be willing to be astounded by what shows up.

The next important consideration is setting aside time for your creative juices to flow. If new ideas aren't forthcoming, then perhaps you aren't allowing enough spaciousness in your life for them to surface. Slowing down and becoming fully present is often the key to accessing this aspect of ourselves. Natalie Goldberg, author of *Writing Down the Bones* and other books on creativity, reminds us that the only place to access creativity is in the present moment. There is nowhere else to escape to in order to tap into our generative self.

One of the most provocative writers and coaches I know is Margaret Wheatley, author of several important books including most recently *Who Do We Choose to Be: Facing Reality, Claiming Leadership, Restoring Sanity.* She encourages us to give up predictability and be willing to be surprised in order to become truly innovative and imaginative. When I teach classes in journal keeping I always invite my students to be willing to discover themselves on the page, to not simply record what they know but to allow what they don't even know they don't know to flow onto the page uncensored.

There are no limits to the creative self...only our own limiting judgments and stifled expressiveness. Since the question is not "Are you creative?" what is the right question? Perhaps you can start with this inquiry: *"How can/do you express your creativity?" Does it reveal itself in your cooking or the way you set the table or the way your house welcomes you home? Is it apparent in the thoughtful gifts you give...perhaps even the way they are presented? Does your creativity come alive through your voice? Does it sing or shape words into sentences that express something essential that is at the core of your being? Or perhaps it is your body that most allows you to reveal your creative core through dance or yoga or the way you run or leap or propel yourself forward through water or snow or on whatever platform or stage becomes available? Or maybe that cleverly creative mind of yours manipulates and tinkers with mechanical things or with numbers or within your garden to discover some new possibility inherent in the nature of it all?*

Dreams Matter

"The future is plump with promise."

~DR. MAYA ANGELOU, AMERICAN POET,
MEMOIRIST, CIVIL RIGHTS ACTIVIST

Isn't the idea of a future that is plump with promise deliciously inviting? Doesn't this notion conjure up all sorts of visual images and fantastic possibilities—especially if you are a dreamer?

Are you a dreamer? I hope so because most of the great things in life actually begin in the realm of the imagination. This book certainly did. Actually, all my books did, as well as all my poems, and my desire to find a way to serve others which is what led to become a life coach. So many of my most important *AHA! moments* have happened when I have taken time to dream.

Building castles in the air isn't a waste of time, as long as you eventually find ways to put a foundation beneath the ones to which you are most drawn. A dream is your vision of something that you deeply care about, that you wish to create or have manifest in the future, and that is worthy of your thought, energy, and resources. This holds true no matter how many years you have been privileged to dwell on this magnificent planet. You are never too old to dream. Actually, nurturing your dreams is essential to nurturing your spirit.

Dreams can arise when life is going along beautifully, because that's when circumstances invite you to expand your horizons further toward what might be viable or reachable. They can also arise because life is not happening at all according to plan, and it is your discontent and restlessness that are fueling your yearning. In either case, if you are a true dreamer, both situations are grist for the mill. If you tend toward reluctance and skepticism, then start small but, by all means, start somewhere.

Those of us who have spent a lifetime stretching and growing into ever more expansive possibilities know that dreams take time, commitment, effort, patience, and a willingness to fall down and pick ourselves up again and again. In the long run, a plump and juicy dream can propel us into those truly significant and sustaining adventures of a lifetime.

Wouldn't it be nice if...? is my favorite dream prompt. A simple way to nudge your thinking in the direction of footloose fantasy is to think about all the *"wouldn't it be nice"* ideas rumbling around in the far corners of your cranium. Allowing yourself to create a plethora of far-reaching imaginings might be the perfect antidote for staying stuck in a relentlessly habitual reality.

Years ago, when I accepted the presidency of Executive Women of the Palm Beaches, members were invited to an overnight retreat so that together we could vision both our own futures and the future of the organization. I actually gave everyone a coffee mug with the words *"Wouldn't it be nice...?"* printed on it as a reminder to take time to sip and savor new possibilities. Attending to one's inner longings is always a good idea. I also gave each member a dream journal with the same inscription to spark the process and get ideas percolating. One important outcome that emerged from that gathering came from Laurie George, who was then the interim CEO of United Way of the Palm Beaches while her organization did a nationwide search for the next executive director. Her *"wouldn't it be nice"* declaration was about how it was time for her non-profit agency to consider appointing a well-qualified female CEO. As a group we responded by encouraging her to put her hat in the ring and promising that we would all campaign on her behalf. And so she did and we did and that year she became the first female CEO. Since then she has done a spectacular job of inspiring countless other women to also step up to their own next level of leadership.

When do you make time to allow your mind wander? Albert Einstein is often quoted as saying, "Imagination is more important than knowledge." Perhaps that's because so much of what makes life marvelous and miraculous happens beyond what we believe can occur based on our logical and linear thought processes. When we allow our thoughts to meander at the far edges of what is solid and factual, possibilities emerge that spark a whole new world of limitless potential.

Here are some questions to perhaps spark your own next *AHA! moment: What is your next best "wouldn't it be nice" idea? What's on your wish list that is begging for your attention? What are you looking forward to and what would be a first step forward in the pursuit of that possibility?*

Castles in the Air

*"If you have built castles in the air, your work need
not be lost. Now put foundations under them."*
~OSA JOHNSON, AMERICAN PHOTOGRAPHER,
EXPLORER, NATURALIST, AUTHOR

C reating castles in the air is a delightful way to begin to lay the
groundwork for anything worth pursuing. Remember the pure joy
of lying in the summer grass watching cloud formations and imagining
all sorts of dreamy possibilities? When did we grow up and stop making
time for dreams?

Here are eight worthwhile steps to consider as you find ways to
build your dreams:

1. *Imagine*—In your mind's eye, create images of possibilities, no matter how wild or far flung they may seem. Remember how as a child,
   watching those clouds go by, you shaped them into imaginary crea-
   tures and objects. We each carry within us this delightful capacity to
   see beyond what is actually there. Rather than pushing those imaginary scenes and scenarios aside, allow them to take shape and expand
   within you.

2. *Don't Censor Your Dreams*—Notice which ideas, desires or fanciful
   wishes repeatedly whisper to you. Observe which ones bring a smile
   to your heart and perhaps even a sense of yearning. Allow yourself to
   remember what you fantasized about as a child, long before you were
   told that your idea wasn't practical or possible. So many of the great
   artists through the ages were told that pursuing a career as an artist

was pure foolishness. Thank goodness they didn't listen. We would live in a very dreary world if they had.

3. *Embellish Your Reveries*—In your early moments of dream incubation, allow yourself to be more and more specific. If you want to become a scientist, think about what you might like to invent that could change the world? Assume that what you yearn for is also yearning for you.

4. *Keep a Bucket List*—These lists have become more and more popular in recent years. We all hold things in our heart of hearts that we would like to experience or accomplish in our lifetime. This is one way to keep them ever-present in your consciousness. While you are at it, do make time to acknowledge those things on your list that you have realized. It helps to recognize the ways you are already living your dreams.

5. *Give Your Dreams Shape through Words*—Write or talk about your dreams, fleshing them out and allowing them to come to life on the page or in your dialogues. Be more and more specific. If you want to become a singer, think about what kind of music you want to give voice to and where you want to perform and who would be in the audience. Sometimes, if you simply talk about what you want often enough, someone or something will turn up in your life to support you in getting the ball rolling.

6. *Be Open to Magic and Miracles*—Remember there is an infinite realm of potentialities filled with what we don't even know we don't know. It is not important for you to decide whether your dream is feasible; focus instead on how dearly you want it. One of the great paradoxes in life is that, more often than not, we cannot see our way through the forest until we are willing to lose ourselves and allow life to find us.

7. *Claim the Universe as Your Partner*—Nothing in life happens in a vacuum. We are all part of this web of life and have access to threads of connection beyond those we can see from where we are standing

right now. As we tug on the strands nearest us, the movement we create ripples out far and wide impacting a larger web we might not yet see.

8. *Get into Action*—As a partner in the process, it is vitally important that you do your part. Make a list of all the things you can begin to do right now, right where you are with the resources you have at hand. *What are you willing to commit to doing...and by when? Whom or what do you know that would help you on your dream journey?*

Live in Awe

no two moments alike
each breath a new beginning
each swirl of cloud patterning the sky
a once in forever configuration...
not two trees alike
each branching their way
skyward in a unique celebration
of light and dark...
no two beings alike
each of us birthed into a unique
space and time
and a particular alignment of moon and stars...

thinking about all of this
it becomes clear that awe
is the only possible response

In my early twenties, during a particularly challenging time, I heard about Transcendental Meditation (TM). TM was touted as a way to stay calm and be at peace with whatever was going on in life. I desperately needed to know more because my inadequate ways of coping and dealing were leaving me both physically and emotionally exhausted. In those days, the whole concept of meditation and mindfulness were very new and considered a bit weird. Even so, I made an appointment and met with a TM instructor. I went through what felt like this rather odd ritual of "receiving" my Sanskrit mantra and trying it out during a brief time of meditative quiet. I was given strict instructions to never speak it aloud or share it with anyone. If I did, its power would be lost. Then home I went. Later in the afternoon, when I dutifully sat down in my very comfy wide red chair to meditate for the second time (the instructions were that the ritual absolutely and positively must be done twice each day to have any impact), I wasn't expecting much. As instructed, I first conjured up in my mind's eye a peaceful scene in nature where I felt safe and relaxed. Sitting there, in front of that imaginary lake, I "allowed" my mantra to come into my mind. I repeated it quietly to myself without forcing anything and then WOW! Suddenly the cells of my body started to vibrate and felt as if they were becoming less solid. I was becoming less solid. The next thing I knew, I had quite simply merged cell by cell with my imaginary lake, with the trees, flowers, and rocks in front of me, becoming one with everything. No kidding. There's no way to really describe all this so that it makes any sense. I was quite simply blown away by the experience. Which is when I panicked and immediately found myself back in my red storybook chair staring out the window at Third Avenue traffic. Yes, of course, that *AHA! moment* changed my life. I had glimpsed something far beyond my ability to comprehend. All I knew was that I wanted more of that expansive experience (which by the way, at least in my case, continues to be a rare occurrence). I have been meditating (off and on) for fifty years now, with only occasional glimpses of the Great Beyond but lots of lovely quiet and soothing moments of ease and peacefulness.

Having shared one extreme of how awe can manifest, I want to be sure to tell you that it is not the only way, nor perhaps even the best way. Looking for the out-of-body awakening can become both distracting and rather disappointing when it doesn't just happen on demand. On the other hand, looking at the sky or a bird or someone's hands or a painting or a potter pulling a bowl into being out of the clay are all breathtaking if we choose to see them that way.

Can you recall an especially blissful moment in your life? Many years ago, at a retreat led by Joan Borysenko (whose books have always found me when I needed guidance and inspiration), she invited us into a meditation where we closed our eyes and mindfully called forth a *holy moment* in our lives—a moment when we felt completely present and serene. The image that came to me was of sitting in a rocking chair late at night with my infant son Reid resting on my chest. His face was *shnoogled* into my neck, and I could feel his warm breath going in and out. In that moment, there was nowhere else to go and nothing else to do. I was absolutely blissful. To this day, when I need to get centered and find inner peace, I always return to that *holy moment* in order to anchor myself and expand my heart to invite in a more tranquil and awe-inspired state of being.

How often to do you allow yourself to be awed by life? It doesn't take much. Whether we contemplate a leaf or look at a living cell under a microscope or watch a sunset or a baby rise up and walk for the first time or view an image of the rings of Saturn (which, miraculously, we are actually capable of photographing), the only intelligent response is AWE. As author Sara Breathnach reminds us, "Life is not measured by the number of breaths we take but by the moments that take our breath away."

On January 1, 2018 my friend, Dena Sisk Foman—lawyer, activist, author of *Only I Define Me*—started a year-long project. She decided to blog daily "about the beautiful things in everyday life that we often miss when we are focused on what is wrong. 'Things' can be words, images, paintings, nature or whatever form my inspiration happens to take that day." Her goal was to create a shift in her own mindset by focusing more on all that is positive, and, hopefully, create a ripple effect. I love this idea and hope that it gains traction. Because I am someone who enjoys journaling and recording memorable moments, I too am taking note of daily glimpses of splendors all around me.

I also have two friends who post photos of the sunrise each morning. Kim Weiss takes her magnificent shots from her balcony overlooking the beach in South Florida. Craig Neal's are taken while on his daily walk around Lake Bde Maka Ska—White Earth Lake—in Minneapolis. I get to "see" these sunrises even when I don't make it to the beach or the lake. *How about you? What do you want to focus on and share with others?*

How well do you pay attention to miracles? Life is a miracle. Everything around us is a miracle. That there is a Creative Force, an Infinite Mind, a Universal Source capable of imagining and creating us and everyone and everything else is reason enough for AWE. As Carl Sagan quipped, "If you wish to make an apple pie truly from scratch, you must first invent the universe." No matter what we as humans become capable of creating and achieving, we are still human and, as William Wordsworth, in *Intimations of Immortality* from his *Recollections of Early Childhood*, reminds us "...trailing clouds of glory do we come, from God, who is our home." I find great comfort and humility in these words.

Consider the words of an indisputable visionary, Albert Einstein, who had the brilliance and perspective to always be AWE-minded. "Those who will pause to wonder and stand rapt in awe will truly live. They will see what others miss. They will feel what others cannot. Life will be for them both exquisite and mysterious." Isn't that exactly what we all hope for—to truly live and feel deeply, to be able to experience the exquisite mystery that is life? Another of Einstein's observations that I have taken to heart is, "There are only two ways to live your life. One is as though nothing is a miracle. The other is as though everything is a miracle." To live life wide eyed with wonder is a challenge and a gift we can give ourselves.

I remember, in the 1970's, seeing Lily Tomlin's performance in the Broadway one-woman show titled *A Search for Intelligent Life in the Universe*. The show was written by her life partner Jane Wagner and in it Lily played various characters or persona. The central figure is Trudy, a very wise *bag lady* who admonishes the audience to "practice AWErobics!" Those words clicked for me and I have been thinking about them ever since. What a delightful practice to incorporate into one's every day.

I wish you many opportunities for AWE. What is yours to do is pay attention, take note, and perhaps even write down the awesome things that appear all around you day after day. *Simply create a page in your journal titled "Moments of Awe" and start writing.*

Embrace the Paradoxes of Aging

*"Oddly enough, the paradox is one of our most valuable
spiritual possessions, while uniformity of meaning is
a sign of weakness.... because only the paradox comes
anywhere near to comprehending the fullness of life."*

~CARL JUNG, SWISS PSYCHOLOGIST AND PSYCHOANALYST

There are ideas that, no matter how contradictory they might seem on the surface, may nonetheless contain truths that are worth considering. What I am discovering—as I grow into and lay claim to my wise woman years—is that I have the capacity to simultaneously hold sacred within me any number of paradoxical ways of seeing and being. This whole concept of *paradox* has provided a steady stream of *AHAs!* for me over the course of many years.

Do More AND Do Less

The first big paradox that comes to mind is that, as we grow into our later years, our focus needs to evolve toward doing both more and less. I know how to work long hours in pursuit of a goal or in order to complete a list, all while exhausting myself in the process. But it no longer serves me to do so, even when there are deadlines looming. It has taken years and tears to arrive at the realization that my big O word—overwhelm—is something that I mostly seem to bring on myself. Here's an essential *AHA!* I have learned the hard way. Just because it fits in my calendar, doesn't mean it fits in my life. My tendency is to be both a people pleaser and a tenacious get-it-done type. As it turns out, this can become a rather lethal combination. The well-known adage, "If you want something done, ask a busy person," comes to mind. That would be ME. Or at least it used to be me. One of the really good things about growing through the decades is that you finally, painstakingly, learn to say "no" as a self-preservation tactic when certain requests are made of you.

Sometimes it's about finding a new rhythm. I have a friend who is a psychologist with a very busy practice. She loves her work and, though in her early seventies, is still thriving at it. What she has learned is how to accommodate to her physical needs by taking longer lunches as well as timely breaks for walks out in the sunshine. One of my best strategies is to take a nap at some point in the afternoon in order to nurture my body and give my brain a break. It's all about discovering one's own *Do Be Do Be Do* rhythm because the paradoxical quest is to do what it takes to stay engaged and relevant throughout one's life.

The book *Pace of Grace: The Virtues of a Sustainable Life* by Linda Kavelin Popov was a lifesaver that landed on my lap just when I needed it most. The premise is that, unless we learn to focus on ease and a certain benevolence toward ourselves, we will suffer consequences physically, mentally, and spiritually. We need "islands of repose, repair, refreshment, and rejuvenation" in order to thrive into our later years. The expression "Don't just do something. Sit there!" could be the perfect mantra for this time in life.

Hurry Up AND Slow Down

A related paradox is that it becomes obvious at a certain point in time that there is only so much time. There are most certainly things that we need to and want to accomplish while we still can. On the other hand, that idea can lead to the troublesome sense that there is no time to waste. Yet, the need to slow down becomes apparent as soon as we start to race through our days and projects. There are lots of things that can go wrong and suffer in the process, including ourselves.

Wayne Muller's book *Sabbath: Finding Rest, Renewal, and Delight in Our Busy Lives* found me seventeen years ago and was another life-saver, just when I was going through two hip replacements. The premise of the book is that if God could take a day off, so can we. Taking a break from the demands of our daily life or even a sabbatical from our career allows us to slow down long enough to work more efficiently and effectively afterwards. Paradoxically, by doing nothing for a while we are ultimately able to do more. Fortunately, before those surgical procedures I worked with a practicing shaman who shared with me several restorative rituals. She also taught me to chant. "I will be gentle with myself. I will love myself." over and over as a reminder to honor my healing journey. There have been many times since then when that chant has served me well.

On the other hand, I recently heard an interview about Dr. Stephen Covey who, toward the end of his life, insisted on the idea of "living life in crescendo" by speeding up so that he could remain significantly involved and at the cutting edge of new ideas. This is another wonderful example of "*both and*" that works for me because here I am still writing books and facilitating workshops and more…at my age!

Hold On AND Let Go

Holding on to our hard-won capabilities and high standards is important. After all, we have worked long and diligently to reach certain levels of expertise and success. On the other hand, over time we learn that expediency also matters. Sometimes getting something done adequately, and in a timely way, matters more than getting it done perfectly but, perhaps, missing the boat.

Holding on to our values is another essential quality of becoming fully human and humane. On the other hand, letting go of any fixed beliefs as to absolute worldviews of how things should be is equally essential for developing our capacity to remain present, kind, and available at all times. Holding to our commitment and doing our part to leave the world a better place requires both tenacity and courage.

Recognizing that there is only so much that we can do allows us to soften our hearts so as to be present, kind, and available to ourselves as well.

Something else to hold on to and let go of is the paradox of keepsakes. Some are treasures, while others just create clutter. We humans tend to accumulate things over time, often squirreling stuff away anywhere and everywhere. Yes, of course, it is important to cherish our memories and our mementos. On the other hand, I am finding great joy in giving away things that I value while I still can so that I witness the pleasure of someone else enjoying them. By the way, now is also a good time to put your house in order and rid it of what you don't want found. Lately, I have been on a campaign to go through and then toss my old journals, which were never meant to be seen by others.

Make New Friends AND Keep the Old

Not exactly a paradox but a conundrum about how to create ample time for those we let into our lives. I remember the importance of having a best friend when I was young. It meant a lot to have a special someone with whom to play, share secrets with, and join forces to face the world through all its confusing ups and downs. I remember as well how hurtful it was when, for whatever reason, something changed or snapped, and that person and I were no longer "besties." Someone else had taken my place or perhaps I had turned my allegiance elsewhere. Those were the black and white years when the concept of more than one best friend was, by definition, an impossibility.

Fortunately, as we grow in years our perspective changes and fortuitous circumstances allow us to gather new friends as we roll along, broadening our horizons along the way. As our hearts expand to embrace first one new friend and then another, we begin to appreciate that perhaps love has no boundaries and to realize that the need to create a rank order of likes (and dislikes) is both unnecessary and unreasonable. There's room enough in our life song for lots and lots of friendship notes, each one, in its own unique way, making the melody richer and more beautiful.

Be a Lifelong Learner AND Lay Claim to Your Wisdom

Staying curious just may be the best antidote to aging. I have come across too many once-interesting people turned into curmudgeonly know-it-alls. As Mark Twain quipped, "The trouble with the world is not that people know too little; it's that they know so many things that just ain't so." Not allowing ourselves to stagnate and stay stuck in what we knew for sure just yesterday is an important life skill that keeps our perspectives fresh and our opinions relevant.

Make time to stretch and grow. There is always something new to discover. The 2017 holiday card from my friends Ione and Gary Wiren shows them holding hands in front of a plaque on a wall that reads, "Boredom is a matter of choice not circumstance." These are the words of writer and philosopher Elbert Hubbard. The quote suits them perfectly. Gary is still out there teaching golf and writing books. Ione has a desk piled high with projects and possibilities of her own. My latest stre*tch-and-grow* ambitions include learning tai chi and homeopathy and, perhaps, finally figuring out how to upload iTunes® music on my phone as well as create playlists (with the help of my grandson because I am so technologically challenged). After that I am thinking about taking a course in collage-making so that I can create art that incorporates words from my poetry with complementary images.

On the other hand, my all-time favorite affirmation is, "I know enough. I do enough. I am enough. Right now." When the going gets tough and I tumble out of balance and into overwhelm, I will sometimes grab my sneakers and hit the road, chanting these words over and over until they sink in and I stop making myself wrong for whatever it is that seems to be out of sorts. At any moment in time, I really do know enough or have access to enough information to do what needs to be done.

Be Content AND Stoke the Fires of Discontent

Contentment is key to developing a sense of satisfaction with one's life and choices. No matter that we have sometimes stumbled, we have made the journey to this moment in time and learned and accomplished much along the way. Hold on to that perspective. On the other hand, resting on one's laurels and becoming complacent about the state of our health, our too cluttered life, or the state of the world is never a good thing. It's essential to stay vigilant about things that matter. Moving from ordinary to extraordinary is sometimes just a tweak away. Don't settle if you don't have to. A corollary to this paradox is...

Develop Patience AND Impatience

Developing patience is an easy concept to understand. To illustrate the equally valid paradoxical idea, I will share a poem that found its way onto my page after a conversation with my friend and colleague Jim Richmond, who told me this *AHA!* story:

"As you grow
older," said the wise grandfather
to his adoring grandchild,
"you will need to learn
impatience."

And the child, believing
his beloved companion
had made a curious mistake or
perhaps it was he who had misheard
the old man's remark,
simply smiled and nodded
and snuggled closer into the warmth
of the good man's presence.

But time is a great teacher and so
many years and journeys later
the man who was that boy
has come to understand
the truth of those words.

Time now seeming so finite
there is precious little to spare
for dolts or dishonest braggarts
nor to dole out to those without
passion or purpose
without compassion or curiosity
nor to make ourselves available to those
so resolute in their misery or miserly
mindsets that they have
closed off to life.

And so the man who was that boy
has come to cherish his grandpa's words
and hold them close
like a compass by which
to navigate the passage of time
and mysterious seas and seasons of life.

Live in the Present Moment AND Be Present to the Past

I believe there is a misunderstanding about the concept of *living in the now* because the present moment is a complex soup and NOW is made up of countless previous moments. Those moments are mostly created by our memories and interpretations of them. Very little of what happens is simply factual (date, time, place, and *exactly* what occurred). I once had to testify at a hearing about an accident I had witnessed. I was totally present in that moment, hands on deck until the ambulance arrived and afterwards at the hospital through surgery and beyond. Yet, two years later I couldn't remember which leg had been injured. YIKES.

Memory is a tricky business. In truth, the past, and our recollection of it, change all the time. In an email exchange my wise and scholarly friend, Lable Braun beautifully summarized this idea by saying, "Each moment contains a dynamic interplay of all three tenses. This present moment contains our present wisdom, which can be used to reframe our understanding of the past and to rewrite it, which then changes our future. The universe is not the fixed point of the present, but the dance of the tenses changing each other in every moment of being."

The Roman Stoic philosopher Seneca warns, "Don't stumble over obstacles that are behind you." Being present to our interpretation of the past allows us to step into this moment and future moments with clarity and power.

The Paradox of Multiple Selves: Both Lived and Not Lived

Our current identity is formed and developed by the many choices we have made. Yet somewhere inside us there are alternate, unlived selves, other possible versions of "me" or "you," that would have blossomed if we had made a different decision or taken a different path somewhere during the narrative thread of our lives. Though these alternate selves may be hidden in the shadow of who we have become, it might still be worthwhile to acknowledge, honor, and embrace them because, by their sacrifices, we have grown into who we are today.

Then, too, beyond these alternate selves there is something more. Rumi speaks of a field "out beyond ideas of wrongdoing and right doing" where we as humans can meet. Countless others speak of it as that spaciousness of mind and heart where the illusion of a separate *you* and *me* dissolves into an appreciation of our common humanity. Perhaps, as we age, that understanding becomes more and more available to us as well.

Exploring the idea even further, what is also true is that within each of us there exist multiple expressions of Self. We are not limited by one fixedly defined personality. We all have numerous ways of being and doing in the world that take center stage and then recede depending on circumstances.

Being Grandma

*"If I knew how wonderful being a grandmother would
be, I would have had grandchildren first!"*

~A POPULAR QUIP/CONFESSION OF MANY GRANDMOTHERS I KNOW

Until you become a grandma, which happened to me rather later in life than many of my friends, you simply don't really know what you don't know. Alex appeared in our family at age eight when Michelle and Reid married. Suddenly I found myself smack in the middle of building block garages for his mini-cars, learning to compete at Boggle®, and playing other games. (Alex has always been a champ at these and would patiently teach me how to play...although I never did master Battleship®), going to the movies to be educated about Jedis and Hogwarts, and trying to grapple with the intricacies of Lego®. (Alex is masterful at assembling the kits in no time flat...while I struggle with putting together a few measly pieces). The only game where I had a chance to hold my own was Scrabble®. To level the playing field, I was not allowed to use three or four-letter words, and Alex picked ten tiles to my seven. One particularly yummy part of our time spent together was, of course, cuddling at bedtime while together we read books on all sorts of fascinating subjects. Wow! I had most certainly been missing out on lots.

I remember a trip Alex and I took to the zoo. Because I am directionally challenged and get lost frequently, it took a while to find our way to the entrance. Alex asked me why I didn't just know where it was (considering how long I have lived in the area). My response was that I had been waiting just for him. His presence in my life finally gave me a worthwhile reason to find and find out about the zoo. Seeing zoos and aquariums and playgrounds with a wide-eyed and enthusiastic child makes all the difference. It also gives us very grown-ups an opportunity to be silly and playful once again, which is a huge added bonus.

Then, a year later our family was blessed again when my grand-daughter, Derby, was born. This is what I wrote on the occasion of her being six weeks old.

you won't remember us
even though you gaze out
from those gorgeous eyes
wide with wonder
but we who are oh so blessed
by your sweet presence
will remember you
newly arrived and all soft
and warm and irresistible
no matter your ongoing
insistence on being endlessly held
and comforted as you find your way
into the light of life

how wise is your instinctive
great and greedy need to be
loved and to feel skin to skin connected
while you navigate the journey
from womb to world and we
your dazzled and devoted onlookers
gladly join together to be your bridge
across the divide between heaven
(from whence you surely came)
and your breath-giving arrival
here upon planet earth

welcome my precious
and already precociously unpredictable
oh so grand miracle of a grandchild
may your days be long and luscious
and filled to overflowing with
the oh so boundless love
and laughter you have so easily
called forth from each and all of us

Over the last eight years Derby, too, has rocked my world as I have watched her grow from infant (who startled me when I first beheld her at the hospital because her lips are as heart-shaped as my mother's had been—as much proof of genetics as I could ever possibly require) to a now rather mature third grader. There have been so many special moments with Derby that have enriched my days. I don't want to do the *grandma thing* and endlessly wax loquacious about all this, so here are just two activities worth sharing. Going to the library has become our special outing where we explore and read and create Lego® scenarios and then make up stories about the characters. I love all this *imagine and pretend* stuff. One time we bought a cuddly Rocket® dog at her school book fair and then took him to the library where we read about him while he, with Derby's enthusiastic help, acted out the activities from the various books. Another favorite pastime has been hanging out in a swimming pool *for hours* while Derby takes on a variety of roles—a mermaid, a gymnast, a champion swimmer, my mother, my big sister, my teacher.

On a Derby Doodle Day
we always always play.
We never ever stop
until at last we drop!!!

Derby is a constant ball of energy. When she finally lays down to sleep SO DO I—*immediately*—happily worn out by the fullness of our times together.

So, what is my most significant personal *AHA!* from being grandma? That I am part of the ongoing flow of life. In another segment I write about my experience in a sweat lodge where I witnessed my lineage—all of my relations who had lived before me—standing hand in hand out in front of me for as far as I could see. On the opposite end of that long line of women, from which I am descended, is Derby, the newest repository of our collective wisdom.

Recently, while engaged in one of those deliciously deep conversations, my friend and colleague Deb Roth observed that one of the most unexpected *AHAs!* of becoming a grandmother is witnessing our own offspring step into their role as parents with tenderness and wisdom and a whole lot more. It's a beautiful sight to behold.

One more observation worth including is that, even though I am a grandmother now, it is also true that once a mother, always a mother. No matter that at some point in time our kids grow up and we need to allow them to be grown-ups and fend for themselves. Still there are those moments when we need to do *the mom thing*—fussing and worrying about them *and* also allowing them to do *the child thing* if need be. Because I'm still MOM, I still send my children away on vacation with an emergency kit of homeopathic remedies and salves and other potions. Last year my very grown up son called from England because he was going through a bout of food poisoning and had been violently ill. He needed to ask what he should do. I told him. He hung up and followed instructions. A few hours later he called back again (obviously feeling better) to ask if it would be okay if he had pizza now! Kids!!!

My Gap Year +

there's a world out there
beyond the limits of
what I have yet allowed in

and there's a world within me
beyond the worries and workaday
confines of my whirring mind

beneath the surface of all that
currently vies for my attention
there is a world worth exploring

I broke my dominant wrist in June of 2016. That accident has been quite a bit more of a game changer than I expected. I needed immediate surgery to repair the damage and then another surgery a year later to deal with some complications and restrictions, the biggest one being that I could not hold a pen to write. This is something of a catastrophe for a writer and poet whose projects always begin to take shape in a notebook or journal. In the March 2017 issue of *AARP Magazine,* memoirist Abigail Thomas writes about taking a quick tumble, breaking her dominant wrist, and becoming quite unable to perform daily tasks like buttering toast, holding a coffee cup, and driving. I know exactly what she means when she says that it was all quite "humbling." Then, two weeks after that cast came off, she broke her other wrist as well. YIKES. (Once again, I can relate, having broken my other wrist years earlier while on vacation.) These are the words, spoken by Abigail to the interviewer, that caught my attention: "Without my right hand, I also couldn't think. Thoughts seemed to make a beeline down my right arm to the hand I write with. With that a dead end…my thoughts were pale and thin." YES, exactly. Me too!

But there's more to it than that. My accident that summer left me feeling both fragile and at risk. I have spoken with several friends who have fallen and broken various body parts in these elder years and they confess the same sense of vulnerability. It takes a lot of courage to push past one's fear, pick oneself up, and step back out into the world, even at half-throttle. Meanwhile, it was a bit of a gap year and a half, some of which was spent simply mustering up the guts and gusto to get up and get going. The thought of tripping and falling again is rather terrifying. I am currently a work in progress finding ways to move past my trepidations and tap into my (b)older self.

On the other side of the coin, I could not have anticipated the benefits of getting off the whirlwind of my merry-go-round life of coaching and doing motivational speaking and workshops, of volunteering and sitting on the Board of Directors of several not-for-profit organizations, of planning and blocking off time for some pleasurable excursions and escapades. All these commitments and possibilities had to be *back-burnered* for a while.

I began thinking about what I could do with this precious time besides a variety of healing modalities and self-care regimens. What could I actually manage within the limitations with which I was dealing? Quite a lot! The biggest project I took on was going through sixty+ years of photo albums and journals, culling from them the best of the best pictures and a broad sense of the chronology of my life and that of my family. I created and scanned collages of key photos and memorabilia that were representational of each year. I put them into three-hole binders and created a second binder (as well as a memory drive) for my son and his family. The *AHA!* for my husband and me was seeing our lives spread out so visually to include the five decades we have lived together and more. It was very rewarding. It turned out to be a sort of life review. As feelings came up, I dictated them into my iPhone "notes" app and then transferred them and printed them out on my computer. Now, having finished this extensive project, there is a pleasing sense of having "arrived" at the completion of this journey through the years and being able to look back at both the main thoroughfares of my life and back roads taken.

Another substantial project I have been working on through this gap year+ and beyond is a commitment to what I call X-Rated Self-Care—Xtreme, Xtraordinary, and Xquisite. I have always walked my talk when it comes to taking good care. Still, this kind of injury at this time in my life has motivated me to be even more diligent and enthusiastic about taking even better care of myself. I am determined to give myself the gift of possibility for many strong, energetic, comfortable, and productive years to come. Of course, there are no guarantees, but I am doing all I know to do to tip the scale toward robust health and well-being *and* to feed my spirit with deep *connectivities* and soul-satisfying reflective respites. I highly recommend this shift in focus to *youngers* and *olders* alike who are reading this.

So, while I literally fell into these gap years, there is now research that shows that a gap year can actually be a good idea later in life in the same way that high school students sometimes take an extended break before starting college and college students do the same before going for further career training. A New York Times newspaper article profiled several older adults who found breathing space and new directions through making time and giving themselves permission to carve out their own gap year.

Are you intrigued by the concept of a gap year...or month...or even a weeklong complete retreat? How might you make that happen?

Becoming a Giraffe

"The fruit of love is service.
The fruit of service is peace."
~MOTHER TERESA, ALBANIAN-INDIAN
ROMAN CATHOLIC NUN AND MISSIONARY

The Giraffe Award is presented each year by the Women's Chamber of Commerce of Palm Beach County. I love the idea that this award is given as a tribute to women who stick their necks out for others. In the spring of 2013, I was honored to be presented with this award. In the afterglow, I began to reflect on my longtime commitments as a volunteer and an advocate. The following poem was one of the first that found its way onto the page as a result of those musings.

college daze
a boy from Bogota
sat down next to me
in Spanish class of all places
such good fortune
with that charming accent
and captivating smile and then
I noticed those dark sightless eyes

"but how will you manage the work?"
I blurted out while staring
at a syllabus of many books
and he inclined his head

toward me and asked
easily with neither pleading nor self-pity
in his mellifluous voice
"perhaps senorita you will
read to me?"

and so I did and so it began
all those years ago
this opportunity for understanding
that what there is to do is simply serve
the person placed on our path with neither
fanfare nor self-importance
but simply because he or she is there
asking or smiling or crying perhaps
it does not matter

the luminous and humble
and tenacious Mother T reminds us
that *"there are no great deeds*
only small ones offered with great
love" and so it is that to love
the world in all its complex wonder
and fullness and pain is the great
and guiding secret to true
happiness and a life worthy
of our time here on earth

Mostly what this poem and the stories that grew from that time are about is the understanding that we are each here to share our gifts and talents and to be of service to others. The first way to do that is simply to notice the person whom *life* puts in our path. Everyday there are opportunities for us to offer a helping hand or be kind to someone—if we are aware enough to recognize the opportunity as it presents itself.

In this particular case, the story behind the story has to do with an accident that I had while traveling by train through Switzerland the summer before, when I was a language student at the universities of Geneva and Lausanne. A tiny metal fragment actually flew into my good right eye (I have had a problematic left eye since I was very young) from an open window on that train and embedded in my iris. Fortunately, a policeman at the next stop directed me to a doctor who removed the sliver and patched my eye to protect it while it healed. Since I don't see well out of the other eye, I was left to deal with a world that looked rather out of focus for several days. My compassion for those with visual challenges expanded while I was groping to find my way around.

Coincidence is sometimes said to be "God's way of remaining anonymous." Somehow, on the first day of that Spanish class, Carlos sat down next to me and our friendship and mutual tutelage began. I practiced my Spanish with him as we went through the course work and he taught me the meaning and nuances of the more complex words and phrases. But there is still more to the story because he had a friend studying at our university who was also blind and also living at the special school for the blind where Carlos was staying. So, I started to read to both of them...and then a third and fourth student, eventually soliciting the help of other students on campus to pitch in and participate. After graduating and moving to New York City, I began volunteering at both Lighthouse for the Blind and the Jewish Guild for the Blind, reading to graduate students there. Because I could read in three languages, I had lots of opportunities to do so. I also started to participate in the effort to record textbooks on tape. It is interesting how one thing leads to another. The work was quite satisfying, and, over time, I met some wonderful people there.

There is another important story and an *AHA! moment* which emerged from receiving that Giraffe Award. Dena Foman Esq., author of the rousing book *Only I Define Me*, was also nominated for the award that year. Afterwards she graciously came up to congratulate me, and my response to her was that she was so deserving of the recognition that I was surprised she had not been chosen. Her words to me, "When one woman wins every woman wins," touched my heart, and I have carried them with me as a mantra ever since. She is so right. As women, each time one of us is honored it simply shines a brighter light on all the good and important things we are out there participating in day after day. I am so grateful to be part of an extraordinary sisterhood of women who are committed to show up, pay attention, and find ways to make a difference again and again. Not all of us get to receive an award, but each of us is blessed with the greater reward that being there for others brings. As Albert Schweitzer observed, "The only people who will be truly happy are those who have found a way to serve."

Consider the ways you have served life. *How many of your big (and small) AHA! moments have arisen from those contributions? And how much joy have you experienced along life's journey by doing so? In what ways are you being called to serve now?*

The Serendipities
of Composing a Life

along the unpredictable way
don't let fear interfere
with the mystery of how
or why things take root
and flourish in their own good time
and at their own perfect pace

surrender instead to serendipity
as you allow what you don't even know
you don't know
to emerge and flower

The gift of living a long life is that there are opportunities to do much and witness even more. We can also reinvent and reinvest in ourselves many times over. I remember reading Mary Catherine Bateson's book, *Composing a Life,* and more recently *Composing a Further Life: The Age of Active Wisdom,* about the ways women tap into so many different aspects of themselves as they take on more and more roles (daughter, wife, mother, grandmother, volunteer, activist, etc.) as well as move from job to job or career to career. Over the years, many of us have woven a very interesting and intricate tapestry out of richly diverse threads of experience.

Among other things, I've worked as a multi-lingual secretary *(because someone knew someone at Union Carbide and recommended me for the job right after I graduated college with a BA in French and Span-ish and no idea what to do)*, as an assistant editor for *Ingenue,* a maga-zine for teens *(again because someone recommended me, and I loved clothes and knew how to put outfits together)*, as an interior designer *(thanks to my mom's friend who helped me with my first apartment and led me to believe that I could do what she did. I wasn't much good at it, by the way.)* before moving on *(impelled by my son's severe asthma)* to become a fer-vent health food advocate, nutritionist, and cooking teacher *(thanks to growing up in the restaurant business and being instilled with a passion for making and eating good food)*…and then moving on to designing and facilitating women's group conversations *(prompted by getting involved with and being inspired by a Bliss Group I belonged to while living in New York City)*…before finally, while in my mid-fifties, settling into a career that evolved to include coaching, facilitating, speaking, and writing *(because, as luck would have it, I met a very talented coach while I was lecturing at a health food store).*

The one thing that stands out for me from this brief summary of *what in the world I have done* is the fact that so much has depended on a string of serendipities along the way. I love Merriam-Webster's definition of *serendipity,* "The faculty or phenomenon of finding valu-able or agreeable things not sought after." I would add unexpected, too. Serendipities are about chance, fate, accidents, providence, coincidence, kismet, and good old luck. They are the profound *AHA! moments and milestones* that are at the core of composing a full and meaningful life.

Here's another story of serendipity. More than thirty years ago, Howie, my rather impulsive and adventurous *cousin-brother* (we were self-declared siblings because of both ideology and inclination), decided we should visit a funky fortune teller in New York City. Definitely not something I would do on my own, but he thought it would be fun to do together. The only recollection I have about the visit was that she told me that I would write "a lot of books." Immediately after that predic-tion, I remember making a snap judgment that this psychic must be a total fraud because I did not consider myself a writer, had never even studied creative writing in college, and wasn't particularly interested in writing.

AHA! but the world works in mysterious ways, and here I am, all these years later, with *a lot of books* that I have authored or co-authored or have participated in by having my works included in anthologies. What I had not taken into consideration when the fortune-teller made her prediction was that I had been seriously keeping a journal since I was about ten years old, had done all sorts of writing, starting in grade school through graduate school, and had, over the years, studied journal-keeping with Ira Progoff, Kay Leigh Hagan, David Whyte, Mark Nepo, and others. I actually knew a lot more about writing than I thought I did. *(How often is that true for you—the ways you downplay or, worse, don't even acknowledge your experiences and accumulated expertise?)*

Fast forward to another serendipitous happening, also involving my cousin Howie, whom I had gone to visit. It was a Friday evening, and so he suggested that we go to synagogue before having dinner. Because the Rabbi there loved my poetry (and because I never go anywhere without a book of my poems in tow), I had a volume tucked into my pocketbook. The Rabbi did indeed ask me to read a poem to the congregation during the services. Afterwards, a young man came up to me and said, "My mother would love your poetry." I thought it odd that he would even know what kind of poetry his mother would like, and I was so touched that I gave him the book. A few weeks later I heard from his mom, who turned out to be Susan Polis Schulz, the founder, with her husband, of Blue Mountain Arts. That was seven years ago, and I have written two books that have been published by them.

Looking further back I can recall all sorts of serendipities that either nudged me one way or another or inspired me to change course completely. Sometimes these happenings appear as the blessing in the challenge, like when, because of my mother's illness and my son's and my own, I turned my energy and focus to learning all I could about becoming more health conscious and conscientious. It was also all the stress of those difficult years that led me to become a runner and to the practice of yoga, both of which have impacted my life. Then came the Wall Street Crash of 1987, which left my husband and me reeling. Even when things slowly got better, Mel and I recognized that the stress of living that kind of life was way too exhausting. So, we made a very bold move and relocated to Florida and a completely different lifestyle. Had we not moved there, I don't know that I would have discovered the whole profession of coaching when I did (which was at the very beginning of the movement to identify, clarify, and codify what it means and what it takes to be a coach). Coaching was such a perfect fit for me that my whole life turned in that direction.

I could, serendipity by serendipity, fill pages and pages with stories about the amazing, kind, sweet, brilliant, audacious, people I have unexpectedly met along the way—teachers, guides, mentors, friends, colleagues, and cohorts as well as a Rolodex of those whose health-wise and healing skills have added immeasurably to the quality of my life. The list goes on, *AHA! moment* by *AHA! moment. Perhaps you too would like to make your own list now?*

Life really does unfold in curious and unanticipated ways. I wish I could find that psychic I met all those years ago to learn what next seemingly outrageous prediction she might now find appearing in her crystal ball. And, right now, I am content with all the ways life has *not* turned out according to plan and curious about all the ways it will probably continue to *not* do so. I hope that you are, too.

You Gotta Have Hope

it's a risky business
this living fully and hopefully
sometimes even frivolously
at the fringes where complacency
no longer satisfies and
curiosity temptingly beckons*

There is an adorable story about a little girl living in a New York apartment who called down to the doorman to tell him that the tooth fairy was coming to see her so be sure to let her in. Smart girl! She definitely had hope, and she understood that it's a good idea to do one's part to help things along. As the lyrics to the song from the show *Damn Yankees* remind us, "You gotta have hope…mustn't sit around and mope." Hope matters AND you have to also do your part.

How often in life are we wishful but not willing to do whatever it is that we can do to up the chances that our outcome will be what we desire? Two years ago, I started sending out an e-Newsletter to a long list of friends, colleagues, and clients with whom I have connected over many years. I am enjoying this creative process because every other week I offer a thought-provoking "Balance Point" followed by *A Question Worth Considering* (because that's what we coaches do—ask good questions, knowing that you have your own best answers). This is followed by an invitation to think about and ideally take to heart *A Shift*

---

* This verse first appeared in Minx Boren, *A Journey to Balance 21 Days to Greater Ease, Energy, and Enthusiasm,* (Boulder, CO: SPS Studios, 2017): Day 17.

Worth Making or *An Action Worth Taking*…because coaching is action oriented. And, as further lyrics to the same song encourage us, "You gotta have heart…miles and miles and miles of heart." No doubt about it. To go the extra mile, you have to bring your passion, sense of purpose, and highest values to fuel your best intentions.

What gives you hope? Think about it. Maybe even make a list. Babies give me hope—so do good teachers, good parents, and good citizenship as well as the willingness to be in an ongoing discourse about what all that means. Good music, art, literature, and beautifully crafted objects give me hope about our infinite creative capacity. Simple and grand acts of kindness and generosity give me hope as do stories of commitment and dedication to anything meaningful and worthwhile. Stories about people who are willing to do what it takes to clean up a neighborhood or the Everglades or corporate corruption give me hope. The Giraffe Heroes Project is devoted to honoring people who stick their necks out for others or for the common good. Reading their bulletins gives me hope. Technology gives me hope. We may yet find a way to recycle all that we use so that nothing is wasted. There are breakthroughs happening in medicine and alternative energy resources that may one day save our bodies from the worst ravages of disease and our planet from the more destructive activities of humankind. Marshall Rosenberg's work on non-violent communication and David Cooperrider's focus on appreciative inquiry give me hope. These are concepts that look at the best of what is possible through human dialogue and of what might be achieved when people collaborate in good faith and with honest intentions. Look at your list and strategize ways to focus on those things that give you hope and boost your spirits.

So why is there so much doom and gloom? Why is it that watching the news of the day or discussing the state of the world or the state of the environment or the state of politics can leave me confused or worse, convinced that things are beyond repair, if I allow my mind to slip into that gray place? Certainly, we live in difficult times. But this has always been true, and the good old days were never really exclusively good. Throughout history, humans have mustered the grace and grit to confront even the most devastating situations of their times. Allowing ourselves to drown in a sea of negativity can whittle away at our hopefulness and at our gusto, leaving us feeling spent rather than focused on spending our human capital in ways that can make a difference. As an elder, I believe that it's my turn to step up and participate in making a positive difference for as long as I possibly can. What that means in terms of actions taken may vary, but my commitment does not.

A pivotal *AHA! moment* in my life occurred while sitting in a synagogue for a Yom Kippur service. Yom Kippur is the Day of Atonement in the Jewish religion, an opportunity to acknowledge those times we have sinned against God or each other—in the sense of being less than kind or humane or failing to do and be the best of which we are capable. I was reading through the prayer book and came across a list of transgressions that included "succumbing to dismay." Those words really caught my attention and invited me to reflect. We all get dismayed sometimes, so why was this so significant? Because to succumb is to give up hope and faith, which, in turn, stifles our capacity to respond with all the love and grace of which we are capable. In the end, hope is a spiritual perspective. When all is in chaos and ruin, hope is the knowledge that, in this vast and infinite universe, we are not alone. Miracles are always possible.

My colleague Harry Hutson co-authored the book titled *Putting Hope to Work* in order to explore its appearance and absence in the workplace today and to make a case for the essentiality of hope to the future of any progressive business. In *Learned Optimism,* Dr. Martin Seligman presents research showing that positive thinking can indeed be learned and that what he calls "flexible optimism" impacts health, creativity, and relationships as well as success at work, school, sports, and just about everything else. One of my current best strategies for dealing with the bleakness of the daily news is to watch a daily TED talk as an antidote and a reminder to stay hopeful.

Remember Pandora's Box, the one she managed to slam shut just before hope could escape? How fortuitous for the human race that we have been given the great gift and blessing of hope, for without it how dreary and tedious life would be. Hope keeps us sane and keeps us striving. Otherwise, we become lost and desperate. As English writer and politician Joseph Addison wisely observed, "The grand essentials to happiness in this life are something to do, something to love, and something to hope for."

"Hope is the pillar of the world." At least so says an African proverb. No matter what is going on, the belief that change is possible and good things can happen is what holds us up and gets us out of bed in the morning. It is hope that emboldens us to direct our best effort toward whatever it is we are facing.

My first question to myself each morning is, *what would make today wonderful?* It's my way of seeding my day with hope. Imagine how exciting life can continue to be at every age if we hold to the belief that we have the ongoing capacity to make a wonderful day, a wonderful year, a wonderful life.

don't get up
not so fast
don't just climb out of bed
not until you are good and ready
good spirited and ready minded
to greet the gift of this day

stay still a moment longer
gather your wits and wonder
let kindness and hope
be the first blessings placed
carefully in your good and ready heart

The words of the poet Emily Dickenson inspire us to, "Dwell in possibility." Yes of course circumstances change, and certain options fall away, but, as long as we draw breath, we can build on all that we have learned and experienced as we continue to be the best expression of our most authentic self. It's never too late to cultivate a healthy attitude, to strengthen our character, to take responsibility for how we show up each day, or for the decisions we make. It is never too late to be kind and loving and to nurture our bodies, minds, and spiritual well-being.

Since hope has been positively linked to everything from physical health to medical recovery to academic achievement to business success and more, it makes great sense to hang on to hope. Hope provides us with a sense of somewhere to go, something to strive for, and the wherewithal to keep going. When I broke my dominant wrist three years ago it would have been easy to give up trying and doing, to give up on all the time-consuming healing practices with which I experimented in order to inch my progress toward better functionality and less pain. But instead, I chose to remain both encouraged and disciplined. There are so many elders I know who are making choices to stay active, determined, and positive in the face of the physical and other challenges that arise year by year.

Perhaps being hopeful, embracing first one possibility and then another, is a basic human instinct, a survival trait. During the most trying times, when life itself is uncertain, it is hope that can tip the balance in our capacity to endure and soldier on. It's certainly a significant asset in terms of living a fulfilling life. The capacity to hope, to dream of new horizons, to imagine future possibilities and successes keeps us vitally alive and engaged in what's going on around us. Consider that the pursuit of happiness granted to us in the Declaration of Independence is, above all, a declaration of and invitation to hope.

By first deciding what we hope for, and then living with that hope at the center of our being, kindling its fire in our belly, and ultimately keeping the flame burning through our attention and intention, life can remain a purposeful adventure for as long as we draw breath. Yes, of course, there will always be inevitable frustrations and times when we fall short or miss the mark, but the very act of pursuit is a demonstration of resilience and courage. Martin Luther King Jr. inspired us to keep on keeping on with these words, "We must accept finite disappointment but never give up infinite hope."

Jack Kornfield is a Buddhist teacher whose newsletter I subscribe to because it keeps hope alive within me. As I was writing this chapter what serendipitously showed up in my email box was Kornfield's declaration of his choice to be hopeful by focusing on the billions of acts of human kindness occurring moment by moment all over the globe. Rather than allowing the big problems of our times to overwhelm us, he suggests that we "honor our human connection and our interdependence with all life." Thank you, Jack, for reminding me of one more way to stay positive.

Finally, consider what Robert F. Kennedy had to say about hope. "Each time a person stands up for an ideal, or acts to improve the lot of others, or strikes out against justice, he sends forth a tiny ripple of hope, and crossing each other from a million different centers of energy and daring, those ripples build a current which can sweep down the mightiest walls of oppression and resistance." Each of us has the capacity to add to the ripple effect in creating a world that works for everyone, including ourselves.

The (b)older I get the clearer it becomes that hope needs to be a choice I make again and again, that the half full glass only appears to be so when I am willing to declare it to be so and live as if it is so…live inside that fullness. What I am committed to doing is to seek out and participate with others who are making the same choice. *Are you?*

PART THREE

VIEW FROM
THE 74TH FLOOR

beyond middle age…a settling in
relaxing into what's so
lovingly
like curling into the well worn
corner of a familiar chair
with a sweet sigh of release
giving oneself permission at last
to rest a while and perhaps savor the journey
memory by precious memory
warm and comforting as hot tea
sipped slowly from a special cup

beyond middle age…a settling down
a willingness finally to be
here and now
staking a claim in the ground
of one's life
feeling the richness of soil made fertile
by simple acts of kindness and
gestures of connection
after all the ambitious racing and chasing
at last a time to catch one's breath

beyond middle age…a settling up
of old scores
as forgiveness finally tips
the scale back toward love
a tallying of that which is
good and fine
mining the vast depths of our days
dipping a bucket into the wellspring
of all we have known and
finding our wisdom is
worth its weight in gold

beyond middle age…a settling
like the old house that has shifted
over time and now rests elegantly yet
ever so slightly askew
tiny telltale cracks and creaks
a confession of imperfections but
also an affirmation of strength and resilience
no matter the disturbances to our foundation
we do not crumble and fall

yes
of course
there are those things
beyond middle age
that we have settled for but
how foolish to dwell in that place
of longing when by shifting
our gaze ever so slightly
the panoramic splendor of a life
fully lived
comes easily into view

An Introduction

I get to be 74. More time to explore.
How amazing.
I get to awaken to this later time
in my life and perhaps still create
the time of my life.

This is perhaps the great gift
of these golden years—
with the proverbial rocking chair
inviting me to relax into my own rhythm
and settle onto a pleasant perch from which to witness
time unfolding more gently now...
a perfect opportunity to generously engage
my senses and my soul.

For those of us who are fortunate enough to live long enough, one day we wake up to the startling realization that we are now the elders. It is not that there is this point of arrival that holds momentous significance but rather that the journey itself has been *and continues to be* rich with experience and meaning.

I spent so much of my life playfully wondering if I were truly a grown-up yet, and then, yikes, here I am! Suddenly (or not so suddenly, because admittedly it has been creeping up on me for a while now), I am beyond seventy years and have entered into what have been called the wisdom years. That means I need to recognize and acknowledge that I am perhaps now a repository of the collective experience of those who have walked this way before me. I recall my experience in the sweat lodge (which I share in the piece titled *Honor Your Lineage)* all those many years ago, and I am filled with a sense of responsibility, awe, and humility.

The other day, I awoke from a dream wanting to ask my mother (who died more than thirty-five years ago) the details about something I was trying to recall, only to realize that the answers resided out there in the ethers somewhere beyond my reach. Yet, as I stayed quiet and simply sat with the question, memories and glimpses of understanding began to surface so that, while the specifics remain lost to me, the essence of that time and those learnings are still available, especially when I am willing to listen deeply.

As I consider the panoramic view from the vantage point of being in my seventh decade, certain things stand out clearly. Above all, what shows up on the horizon is the understanding that, while I am committed to shaping these elder years into a precious opportunity, rich with experience and exploration, I do not want to turn them into a race to the finish line—so much to do and so little time left. I do not want them to become something else that I need to accomplish...perfectly!

I came of age as part of the "superwoman generation" when women's lib was gaining momentum. I truly believed that there were no limits to all that I could accomplish if only I would continually give it my all with determination and grit. So, no matter how much I did, there was always more I believed I could, would, and should be doing. No matter how much I learned, there was always more I had to know before it would be enough. I spent endless time and energy trying to do, be, and achieve it all, exhausting myself by taking numerous courses and taking on countless roles, projects, and commitments. Enough was never enough.

I'm not exactly sure when I started, in minute and subtle ways at first, to change. Perhaps it began when I first learned how to meditate and quiet my mind. Perhaps it began soon after my son was born. I was so sick...and so was he...and so was my mother...and both of my in-laws. I had to learn to get through one day at a time. I learned to be grateful for quiet moments and reprieves. I learned to appreciate each small step toward health.

It became more and more clear that what mattered most was how I coped with each moment. How much heart and mindfulness I brought to each challenge was the greatest, and sometimes the only, gift I could offer. Coping led to acceptance, and learning acceptance has taught me to do my best to focus on being fully attentive to the moment at hand.

I do not want to suggest that I have ever come close to mastering this capacity for full presence. My choices over time most often exhibit a pattern of two steps forward and one step back. A few years ago, the opportunity to learn this lesson yet again showed up when I took on the presidency of a major women's organization in Palm Beach County. I was both honored and daunted by what this commitment involved. Having said "yes" to the challenge, I spent three years (as president-elect, president, and then immediate past president) giving it my best shot. It was an extraordinary experience. I learned more than I could have imagined and was amazed and humbled by all the support, encouragement, and hands-on help I received throughout my tenure in office. I wouldn't trade that experience for anything. Stepping down from that position just before I turned seventy, I also recognized that I wanted to create a different way of being and doing for these later years.

Books are among my greatest teachers. The right book somehow seems to land in my lap precisely when I need it most. Just as my tenure was ending, I read Linda Popov's book, *A Pace of Grace*. Her story and philosophy resonated deeply and provided me with a very enlightening *AHA! moment*. I too know all too well how to work long hours and exhaust myself (for good and also not so good reasons), but I know that intense level of drive no longer serves me. In the wake of my presidential term, I began to ease up on the pace of my activities. To be honest this is partly because I tire more easily now and lose the ability to sustain a marathon of concentrated focus to the extent that I once could. Actually, when I ran marathons, I loved the challenge and thrill of those races. But that was then, and this is now. I am finding, admittedly sometimes somewhat reluctantly, that now is the time to slip into less driven and demanding days and ways.

As a side note, looking back, what I remember about running those marathons is that the last five to six miles required all the grit and gusto I could muster. In actuality, I made it through that grueling last leg by just putting one foot in front of the other, watching the road as each foot landed, hyper-focusing on what was immediately in front of me and not looking up to seek out the distant finish line. I knew I made it only when I saw the painted yellow stripe on the ground as I stepped over it. Isn't it true that sometimes life is exactly like that? The only way to make it through is one small step at a time.

Another book that landed in my lap just when I needed it was *The December Project,* written by one of my favorite authors, Sara Davidson. In 2008 I read another of her thoughtfully provocative books titled *Leap: What Will We Do with the Rest of Our Lives?* It came at the perfect time to inspire me to reach toward a next important opportunity, rather than choosing to *play it small.* This time, Sara was invited by Rabbi Zalman Schachter-Shalomi, founder of the Jewish Renewal Movement and author of *From Aging to Sage-ing,* to join with him in a conversation exploring life's greatest mysteries. The central thesis of their book focuses on recognizing the importance, at a certain point in one's life, of taking the time to contemplate the whole of one's journey and to recognize the cohesiveness and the rightness of how it has unfolded. To do so requires TIME. It is essential to not rush through the process. A life review such as they are suggesting requires both spaciousness and an open-hearted, open-minded gentleness if it is to be meaningful and yield the richness of understanding that is hoped for. Ultimately it is about the desire to know one's *Essential Self*—the motivating force behind not only all that we choose but also how we interpret all that we witness and experience.

I am discovering that the view from beyond age seventy is a fascinating one. There is a term—the percolation effect—which refers to the rising of new awareness to the surface of one's conscious as pieces of information come together in unique and unforeseen ways. When we stop trying to explain things from a certain predetermined or pre-formulated perspective, and simply surrender, we become an invitation to receive through intuitive whisperings, unexpected understandings, inspirational awakenings, creative sparks, miracles, and grace. This does not mean we lose all discernment and discrimination. It does mean that we hold ourselves like the scientist who has completed years of education, research, and experimentation in order to achieve an understanding or particular result. Finally, he or she receives the sought-after realization in a dream, while walking, or, like Archimedes, while taking a bath.

Nowadays I indulge in taking more baths, walks, and naps. I have also taken time to pull out old journals and photo albums to jog my memories while simultaneously assembling year-by-year summary pages.

How about you? What would serve you now? Are there things you would like to review or research or reminisce about so as to reconnect with the bigger picture of your life journey? Or perhaps there is some next great adventure or project that you can see clearly on the horizon? Or maybe the pull for you now isn't either/or but rather to do both?

In any case, please don't delay. As the sages of all ages remind us, now is the only certain time we have.

Pearls

how fascinating it is
that so many gritty morsels of life
so many moments and mistakes
I wish I could have wished away
have held within them some tiny kernel
or crumb or seed of possibility
for something else to blossom

As we grow and develop and experience LIFE, it seems that each human increasingly becomes a repository of precious pearls of wisdom. Writing this book and gathering an abundance of rich ideas culled from the vantage point and blessings of being alive for many years got me thinking about pearls…and pearls of wisdom…and more. First of all, my mother, when she died many years ago, left me her double strand of pearls that I have continued to wear and cherish for a very long time now. One of the things I have learned about pearls is that they want to be worn, need to be worn, and that their luster increases when they are brought into the light of day rather than left tucked away somewhere. The same holds true for ideas, inklings, and inspirations. Tucked away in corners of my mind, they serve no one, least of all me. What good is it to spend a lifetime gathering up the lessons and glimpsing the gifts of one's experiences unless they are exposed to the light and their luster allowed to shine through?

Pearls are precious. Here is some fascinating, albeit technical, information. Something so perfectly beautiful is actually produced as the result of an irritation caused by a foreign substance entering the shell of an oyster or other bivalve mollusk. In the case of a natural pearl, the microscopic intruder is generally a parasite while cultured pearls are the response to an implant of a tiny piece of mantle tissue (called a *graft*) from a donor shell into a recipient shell. In either case, a pearl sac forms to cover the irritant. The unique luster of a pearl actually depends upon layer upon translucent layer of a minute crystalline form of calcium carbonate and complex proteins called conchiolins that are deposited in concentric coatings around the foreign object. This process results in a spherical or otherwise shaped object with a certain iridescent quality of reflection, refraction, and diffraction of light. The thinner and more numerous the layers within the pearl, the finer the luster. This too seems to be true for pearls of wisdom. Often, the most bothersome bits and pieces of ideas and experiences become the "irritants" that won't go away, requiring that we turn our attention to them again and again to puzzle our way through to some deeper level of understanding. Then, when we have accumulated layer upon layer of wisdom, we need to stop just ruminating and have the courage to bring our best ideas out of hiding in order to observe how they fare when exposed and illuminated.

For centuries, pearls have been used for adornment. They have been sewn onto regal garments, incorporated into headdresses, and set into rings, earrings, clips, and necklaces. When individually stunning pearls are carefully chosen and strung together in artful ways, the effect of the whole becomes more than each individual pearl. This idea likewise has merit when it comes to pearls of wisdom. One might be interesting *and*, when gathered in a thoughtful and harmonious way into a larger context, they can become even more remarkable and valuable.

All this provides much philosophical grist for the mill—the fascinating process by which something gritty becomes a pearl...something of great value...and then something that we cherish...and share. In ancient times, pearls were also used as a commodity of exchange for trading and bartering. This, it seems, is true of pearls of wit and wisdom, considering the conversational exchanges that they can spark.

When I think of pearls, I also think of my senior high school English teacher who required that each day, in exchange for being admitted to her class, we had to write a 350-500-word essay. Not just any old bunch of words *kerplunked* onto the page, but something thoughtful and provocative and carefully assembled so as to be worth the time it would take her to read each of our submissions. I used to labor diligently over those nightly assignments, all the while bemoaning how much time they took. Yet, it is because of those homework obligations that I actually learned to shape my ideas into something substantive, coherent, and cohesive...like a string of pearls. No matter that my early attempts were not always gracefully (let alone brilliantly) strung together. Everything starts somewhere, and, with trial and error, my attempts improved over time.

Having spoken about my mother's double strand of pearls, I want to mention that, more recently, I rediscovered, in an old jewelry box of hers that I had put away high in a closet, yet another strand of pearls. This one is opera length and made of differently shaped baroque pearls. Someday, both of these will be passed on—one to my granddaughter and the other to the wife of whomever my grandson marries. This thought brings me great comfort and joy, as does the thought that the pearls in this book might find their way out into the world and that those who take the time to actually explore them and turn them over and over in their own mind's eye might be inspired by doing so. My hope is that they will be valued enough to also be worth revisiting and sharing.

The word *pearl* has become a metaphor for something rare, fine, admirable, and valuable. The ideal pearl is sometimes thought to be perfectly round, but, in actuality, natural pearls rarely are and generally come in many shapes. Those that are most highly prized are found in the wild, and there are also cultivated or cultured varieties that have real value. Pearls are not always pearly white. They also come in various shades of creams, pastels, and earth-tones. Like most things in life, there is no one right or best choice, and there are lots of variations and permutations...just like pearls of wisdom.

How about you? When have you taken time to think about your precious pearls of wisdom, gathered throughout however many years you have been alive? And how and when have you blessed others by sharing them? And whom might you bless right now by offering an appropriate gem?

The Tapestry of Life

Corrie ten Boom
Dutch Christian, Holocaust survivor
rescuer of many—
likened life to a tapestry neatly woven
by all outward appearances
on the one side
and a chaotic expanse of loose threads
and random knots
on the other

this works for me
there is beauty to be found
on both sides of the cloth
the assemblage of carefully laid threads
on the one hand
and the profuse energetic explosion
of uncontainable aliveness behind the scene

Have you ever noticed how we, as humans, want so much to be in control that we sometimes desperately try to cling to a certain sense of orderliness in our lives, no matter the truth of the circumstances? Yet, if we liken our lives to a cloth that we are doing our best to carefully embroider, what is also true is that, as we turn that cloth over, there is a certain chaotic randomness of threads that greets us on the other side. Seeing this, it might take a while to resist the need (and unnecessary expenditure of time and effort) to tidy it all up, and, instead, embrace all the ways that this tangle has contributed to the pattern that has emerged on the side that the world gets to see.

So it is with growing into our wisdom years. After all the comings and goings, beginnings and endings, uplifting moments and difficult challenges of a life fully lived, there comes a time when a certain wholeness emerges—even as we paradoxically recognize a certain inevitable randomness that has had its unseen impact as well.

What I am discovering as I grow into and lay claim to my *wise woman* is that I am developing the capacity to hold sacred within me the whole of it. This includes those things hoped for, worked for, and embraced, as well as those that found their way into my life unexpected or unbidden, whether by fate or fortune or the random whimsies of the universe.

We live in distressing and chaotic times. Perhaps this has always been true, but when we reach a certain vantage point of years those difficulties seem to loom larger than ever. Yet, seeded within the challenges we face are new possibilities waiting to be discovered and developed. What is required of us is both attention and intention—the ability to pay attention and stay present to what is going on (while doing our best to steer clear of the drama and negativity that can diminish our enthusiasm), and our intention to remain engaged, productive, and resilient, especially in stressful circumstances.

As we move toward our later decades, there remain before us the ongoing challenge and choice to stay involved and embrace each moment with all the hope, hardiness, wisdom, passion, and joy we can muster.

Age Softens Us

life is feeling softer now
as I learn to abandon grand plans
and long-term goals complete
with all sorts of fancy strategic plans
and simply settle
into the next right thing…
with this ripeness of age
feelings of overwhelm are giving way
to the easy presence of just here just now
and just this next right thing

One of the blessings of growing older is that the gift of years can offer a more panoramic and holistic vantage point than the perspective available to us in the midst of the daily comings and goings and doings of life. We can see beyond the small struggles and petty hurts that keep us feeling separate. We can recognize that those events we once considered ominous and insurmountable were indeed not as catastrophic as we once believed they would be. We learn that the wisdom behind the oft-spoken words *"this too shall pass"* turn out to indeed be true.

Juan Carlos is an intelligent and tech-savvy guy. He is also quite wise, which I appreciate especially because he is quite a bit younger than I am. I first met him because he is a friend of my son. It's interesting how blessings and the right teachers can arrive in your life just when you most need them. Actually, I originally invited JC to stay with my husband and me for a few weeks during a tumultuous time of upheaval in his life. He needed a safe and loving place to land for a while. He was so easy to have around, and we had such great philosophical conversations at all sorts of odd hours that his company was delightful. He continued to live with us for about three years during a time in his early thirties while he was reinventing his life. As it happened, I was just learning how to use a computer way back then. He provided both sanity and perspective about the whole challenge of learning something that was so complex, foreign, and intimidating to me. I recall the many nights I would knock on his door to tell him that I had just lost—the computer had just gobbled up—whatever piece I was writing and I was upset at the prospect of having to recreate all the good ideas I had typed onto the page. Every time, JC would come to the rescue. While I paced and fretted, he would, step by careful step, do whatever it was that he did to retrieve the lost document. Always he would say to me, *"Paciencia senora. Paciencia."* I admit that I was rather slow at learning that particular lesson, but all these years later those words come back to me again and again. I no longer panic quite so easily. Of course, I've learned to also take more precautions to save my work along the way and to have multiple ongoing back-up systems (also thanks to JC). But patience is a virtue worth cultivating. It softens us.

I would like to believe that age in general softens us, not just our bodies but also around the edges, smoothing out and easing up our ways of being and doing. While physical flexibility may decrease over time, my hope is that our willingness to bend with circumstances and accommodate to the values and viewpoints of others might more than compensate for these shifting physical limitations.

Could it be that, having lived long enough, we pass over some invisible threshold where we are able, at last, to abandon absolutes in favor of the infinite ways of being and knowing that we come to appreciate in one another? The ancient American Indian wisdom of walking a mile in the moccasins of another before passing judgment comes to mind. Perhaps its relevance lies in having reached an age when our own feet sometimes ache, requiring self-compassion and TLC in order to go the extra mile or even just find our way to a place of rest.

Could it be that we hold within us the capacity and inclination to become more reasonable and accepting with each passing year? Could it be that life teaches us through both the blessings and burdens that come our way, the fullness of what it means to be human?

And could it be that at some point in time we recognize that absolutes aren't real... that "always" and "never" don't actually exist in the real world? When I was president of Executive Women of the Palm Beaches, I sought advice from each of the past presidents, who made themselves available in order for me to learn about how things were done in the past. Former president Terry Gearing offered this rather intriguing piece of wisdom—yet another *AHA! moment.* "If you think we have never done it that way, the truth is that we almost certainly have. And, if you think we have always done it that way, that too is equally unlikely." What experience has taught me is that when I hear the words "always" or "never" my mind shifts to high alert. My *internal warning system* somehow knows better than to allow absolutes to slip through the cracks of my awareness without a soul-searching reality check.

Life reminds us again and again of how fragile and fleeting it all is. *While this might at times cause us great pain and an expanding sense of loss, does it not also gift us with an even greater appreciation for each and every moment that is ours to live? Does it not also offer us opportunities to become more and more gracious about how we see things whole?* I would like to believe so.

Embrace Change

embrace change
don't hold too tightly
to always *and* never
rules are made
to be relinquished
as time shifts and shimmies along
and new vistas
come into view

Growing into our wisdom years is, above all, about becoming vulnerable in the face of change rather than resisting it. This is not so easy. What about the times when I rather like things just the way they are? Having worked diligently to get my life in order, to master certain competencies, to move past certain limitations, it just doesn't seem fair that things have to alter and shift. But, no matter my resistance, things do change. As the oft quoted words of Allen Saunders, popularized by songwriter John Lennon in "Beautiful Boy," remind us, "Life is what happens to you while you're busy making other plans."

In a recent coach seminar I attended, the presenter spoke about the necessity of working with clients on the skills they will need to master so that they remain relevant and productive three years from now. YIKES…just three years!?! The world changes so quickly nowadays that all too soon our current abilities simply won't pass muster. I know how frustrating this can be. Just as I become familiar with my current word processing program, the next *improved* version moves icons around while adding new bells, whistles, and procedures. The same is true with the financial tracking programs in my computer. My accountant is constantly having to upgrade my skillset so I can keep up.

Understanding that what brought us to age fifty or sixty or seventy, no matter how brilliant our strategies and heroic our efforts to manage everything, is not what will get us to eighty or ninety. Like the bamboo tree that bends with any breeze, those who are flexible, curious, and receptive are less likely to be toppled by the winds of fortune and the latest and greatest technological advancements. Consider too that a painting is always both exactly the same and entirely different every time you look at it. It makes good sense to keep looking with fresh eyes.

According to Buddhist teaching, the nature of life is impermanence. What causes us to suffer is simply our refusal to accept this fact. Have you ever seen Buddhist monks sit for hours creating magnificent and intricate sand paintings only to blow them away after they are completed? I don't know about you, but it breaks my heart to see something so beautiful destroyed. Yet the immediacy of the learning it demonstrates is magnificent. I remember building castles in the sand as a child, and part of the fun was racing against the tide to complete them before the waves washed them away. There's a lesson to be learned here. If only I could tap into that youthful playfulness in my adult years and not cling so tightly.

At the extreme ends of a long continuum of how we as humans deal with change are two diametrically opposed strategies. First, because of our great fear of the unknown and of being out of control, we cling to the status quo—the safe and familiar—with all our might. An alternate strategy is to simply let go and *go with the flow* of life. Each possibility involves our "energy." But clinging requires the greater expenditure; it can be frustrating and fruitless, and often leaves us feeling stressed and exhausted. On the other hand, allowing ourselves to be carried by the currents of life's changing tides can leave us refreshed and renewed. To *be in the flow* means to be totally present and responsive to what's going on around us, even as we simultaneously continue to thoughtfully direct our energy toward our intentions and commitments.

Staying in the flow is a lifelong excursion. Our task is to surf the waves that come our way while remaining awake and aware, balanced and centered, prepared and open to possibilities. *And so how might you allow change to energize you by preparing for and managing your response to the inevitable shifts that life brings?*

No matter how hard I have tried to stay safe and in control, to protect myself and those I love from anything I perceive as negative, life happens. Now at seventy+ years old, the inevitable changes that accompany the aging process have become a constant reminder to not struggle endlessly against what is so, but rather find a flexible rhythm that allows me to ride the waves more gracefully.

As feminist, journalist, and social political activist Gloria Steinem so wisely said, "The art of life isn't controlling what happens, which is impossible; it's using what happens." That seems like as good a strategy as any to begin to embrace change as the very sum and substance of life. By finding ways to welcome the endless stream of new challenges and possibilities that are constantly arising, we can learn to approach them with a sense of anticipation and curiosity rather than dread. Again, easier said than done but essential none the less.

Beginning with a strong and resilient body seems like an excellent foundation for supporting change. By committing to our own diligent self-care—taking time to eat properly, get adequate rest, and exercise to build strength and stamina—we can fortify ourselves to meet life's demands as they arise. This is not about striving for perfection, which only sabotages one's best efforts. It's about doing enough and feeling well enough to do what we hope to do. So, too, by cultivating a certain resilience of mind, we can sustain ourselves through an ongoing journey of discovery and learning as a way to *grow with the flow* and to participate fully in whatever is occurring within and around us.

Living successfully is about making good choices. As things inevitably change, we can continue to engage in an introspective inquiry into our own personal truths, values, and sense of purpose. To access this cognizance, no matter the turbulence in life, there is always available within us a center, still-point of peacefulness. Meditation, journal writing, prayer, simple rituals, yoga practice, and deep breathing are all ways to tap into a sense of focused presence from which to navigate our options.

Finally, it is of paramount importance to recognize and respect that none of us is wise enough alone. We must seek out the companionship and support of others to help steer our way through high and low tides. Beyond our human connection, perhaps now is also a good time for us to deepen our understanding of and connection with the Divine as a way to sustain and comfort us. I love the idea that prayer is when we talk to God and meditation is when we listen. I find that I am doing more of both now.

AHA! While our unfolding story is about what actually happens while we are occupied with first setting our sights and declaring our intentions and then planning and plotting and plodding our way along, it is within those very twists and turns and surprises that we may be most blessed and enlivened by the magic and mystery of it all.

Coping with Sadness

When the time comes
and the devastating news
or dreaded diagnosis is spoken aloud
and the earth gives way beneath
our weary feet
how does one begin to steady oneself
to not lose hope
and to find the next graceful
*or awkward or tremulous step?**

*H*ow do we learn to be with sadness and not run from it? How do we plunge into the depths of our grief without losing ourselves there?

If we live long enough we have, by necessity, found our own unique ways to cope with the bitterness and disappointments of life. At some point in time, if we are wise, we mature enough to accept and take responsibility for our life—the whole of it—both the good and the less than positive choices and happenstances alike. We recognize *what's so* as well as *what might never be so* and move forward as best we can.

Duke Ellington elucidated his creative process by saying, "I merely took the energy it takes to pout and wrote some blues." I believe he touched upon a great truth in understanding that the key lies in not fighting against all that emotional energy, but rather channeling it in

---

* An original shorter version of this first appeared in Minx Boren, *Healing Is a Journey: Find your own path to hope, recovery, and wellness,* (Boulder, CO: Blue Mountain Arts, 2014): Pages 33–34.

some useful direction. In the course of a single life we must each confront so much sadness and deal with so much loss as adversities touch our lives and the lives of those we love. We have all known times when simply putting one foot in front of the other has seemed a monumental task in the face of great tragedy. Yet, somehow, we do. By summoning our own inner strength while also relying on the support of others, mostly we manage and make it through.

MADD (Mothers Against Drunk Driving) was started by Candice Lightner, whose child was killed by someone driving while under the influence of alcohol. The whole concept of micro-lending was started by Muhammad Yunus, founder of the Grameen Bank, who was saddened by the great poverty he witnessed and frustrated because, in spite of his Harvard education, he could not improve the lot of his own people in Bangladesh. Good people everywhere have done great things because they found a way to feel their sadness and use it as grist for the mill rather than fodder to feed their sense of futility.

Sometimes I have used up the energy of my sadness dwelling on all that is wrong, unfair, bitter, or mean-spirited. I have ranted and wretched until there was nothing left inside. Other times I have been able to hold my sadness more softly, allowing it to speak to me in its own voice without censure. The blessing has always come when, somewhere beyond the grieving and suffering, some small glimmer of light or lightness has invited me to take a first small step. Beyond the drama and distress, I am shown some small glimpse of what might be possible. Beyond the pity and the pain, I am moved by something useful and good that has the capacity to enliven me once again.

There are all these quotes that live in my head, providing me with countless *AHA! moments*, because they are words that have inspired me along the way. A friend captured my attention with this observation, "The challenges and aches and pains of aging can be very serious and very difficult, but they are rarely interesting." I do the best I can to remember this wisdom when I am about to launch into some body-ache inventory or some story of current loss or lack. It serves no one, least of all myself, to dwell in that perspective. Here's another quote I mindfully carry within me as a reminder. While it has been attributed to Eleanor Roosevelt and others, an Internet search tells me that this is actually a Maori proverb. "Turn your face toward the sun and the shadows will fall away behind you."

Beyond simply turning toward the sun or the music or the sound of laughter or an invitation to share a meal or a moment with someone—all of which are gently impactful ways to ease out of sadness or be distracted from it, at least for a little while—there is another skill that those of us who are determined to grow (b)older with grace and dignity and grit can do our best to focus on. Let me share yet another wise epigram, this one attributed to the Sufi tradition: "When the heart grieves over what it has lost, the spirit rejoices over what it has left." So, in the tough times—the times of loss or lack, of disappointments or difficulties, of downturns or upheavals—perhaps the most reliable immediate strategy, beyond being willing to simply acknowledge and be with what is so in the moment, is to search within ourselves again and again for that which we can still truly be grateful.

I know someone who went through surgery for lung cancer several years ago. Months later she began coming to spin class again, and so I asked her how she was coping with no longer being capable of keeping up at the same level of performance as before. Her answer, "This is my new normal," was truly a magnificent statement of acceptance and courage. I watch those of us who are experiencing the inevitable aches and physical limitations that seem to be part and parcel of growing older, admiring the grace and gentle humor I witness all around me. Certainly, there is sadness associated with the shifts and changes that time brings but there is also thankfulness for and a certain curiosity about all that might still be possible, for as long as we still draw breath.

Celebrating Friendships

Let's celebrate
today
like every day
as another anniversary
in the expanding blessing
*of our togetherness**

If there is one thing that those of us who have lived long enough know with absolute certainty, it is that our friendships make all the difference. They nourish our spirits, inspire our minds, and soothe our hearts. When the going gets tough, our closest companions are the ones who help us deal with both the stressors and practicalities of responding to the challenge. Friends are a wellspring of joy, comfort, and wisdom from which to draw sustenance. To quote the French-German theologian, writer, humanitarian, philosopher, and physician Albert Schweitzer, "Sometimes our light goes out but is blown into flame by another human being. Each of us owes deepest thanks to those who have rekindled this light."

Every night before turning out the lights, I reach for my journal to write down three good things that happened that day. This is a very satisfying and comforting ritual I have been practicing for many years. What I have observed is that what I am most grateful for are the ways

---

* Excerpts of this chapter along with the full poem first appeared in Minx Boren, *Friendship Is a Journey–A Celebration of Deep Connection and True Sharing*, (Boulder, CO: Blue Mountain Arts, 2016).

my friendships, and even the smallest of interactions with acquaintances or strangers, are a blessing to me each and every day.

"Let us be grateful to people who make us happy;
they are the charming gardeners who make our souls blossom."
~MARCEL PROUST, FRENCH NOVELIST, CRITIC, ESSAYIST

The benefits of writing down what we are most grateful for has been thoroughly researched in the field of positive psychology. But there is this caveat: it's not enough to simply write down, "I am grateful for Mary or John's presence in my life." It's essential to take it a step further and say specifically why the gift of their presence is a blessing *that day*. For example, "I am grateful that Mary or John showed up with hot soup or pizza…or telephoned at the perfect moment to check in on me…or invited me to join her or him for an outing…just when I needed it most." Even a stranger can evoke gratitude worth noting. For example, "I am grateful for the cashier who took time to smile and chat with me while ringing up my purchases." By being precise about the feelings of gratitude generated by particular experiences, this ritual can remain fresh and relevant.

I have also noticed that, while sometimes my gratitude is all about the way someone has shown up when I needed them, other times it is simply about acknowledging good times shared. On other occasions it is about the privilege of being asked for help by a friend in need or simply seeing, before even being asked, an opportunity to bring joy or to be of service to another.

A third essential aspect of the "three good things" exercise is taking a moment to note *why* this particular good thing happened. This allows us to see our own participation in the goodness of our lives, whether because we actively reached out or took a stand or a step forward or simply expanded our horizons to recognize the beauty around us. Nowhere is this more vital than when reflecting upon our friendships because of the give-and-take aspect of true relationships. Of course, sometimes there may be more give than take, *and* sometimes the opposite is true. The key is to acknowledge how who we are and the ways we show up make all the difference in the quality and richness of our connections.

Especially if you are fifty+, I don't need to tell you how important friendships are. You have had ample time to grow and thrive and find meaning in your life through these bonds of caring and sharing. Still, it's important to note that, while relationships become increasingly comfortable over time, the challenge can be that this same familiarity allows us to slip into the danger zone of taking someone for granted, of making the assumption that the connection will remain rich, gratifying, and solid—no matter whether or not we continue to tend to it quite so lovingly and appreciatively. We need to remember to show our gratitude by *fluffing the feathers* of our friendships in order to assure that our friends *feel* our appreciation for who they are, what they do, and how much of a difference they make in our life and in the world. While this may be a particularly feminine approach, men too will benefit from finding ways to *high five* and *praise* their best buddies.

When I turned seventy, I decided to go on a *friendship journey*. I spent several months taking brief trips in order to visit my very dearest friends, some of whom I have known for more than fifty years. I spent precious time with each one, sharing what I most love, appreciate, and celebrate about them. I presented each with a handwritten note, actually "listing" those key points, so that they would be able to keep my words close as a reminder of how unique and awesome they are in my eyes. In every case, these occasions for deep connection were magical and meaningful. My husband's version of this type of opportunity for connection when he turned seventy was a special golf trip away with some guy friends. While our *styles* differed greatly, we were each richly rewarded by the experiences.

I have heard it said that it's never too soon to share love and appreciation because none of us knows when it might be too late to do so. I approached turning seventy as a milestone worth noting—a time to pause for deep reflection about my life so far, as well as an opportunity for thoughtful introspection about *what now* and *what next*. What I know for certain is that, as I move beyond that momentous occasion, my friends continue to be at the core of what keeps me strong and makes every step of the way more satisfying.

Are there friends you would like to carve out special time to be with? Are there those to whom you would like to express appreciation? To whom will you reach out and connect with today?

There is of course no time like the present because now is the only moment that's real.

See Your Beauty

the elder years can be a time
of such radical radiance
and so it is that as I grow
older I seek out graciously loving
eyes and the kind of light
that allows my beauty
to shine through softly

"**B**eauty is in the eye of the beholder." This brilliant piece of wisdom, first recorded in the book *Molly Bawn* by Margaret Wolfe Hungerford, is a poignant reminder of the subjectivity of the whole concept of attractiveness and attraction. Let us also take into consideration the corollary idea that the most important beholder is you!

Given all the air-brushed images of gorgeous models on billboards and in magazines, it's no wonder that we sometimes feel that we don't measure up to this idealized version of beauty. Yet I remember the actress Jamie Lee Curtis allowing *More Magazine*, in 2002, to photograph her at home in plain Jane underwear, without benefit of stylists, flattering camera angles, make-up or retouching. Her honesty made a profound impression on me. Consider this remark by a well-known fashion model: "I think women see me on the cover of magazines and think I never have a pimple or bags under my eyes. You have to realize that's after two hours of hair and makeup, plus retouching. Even I don't wake up looking like Cindy Crawford." Oprah too has been generous in giving us a backstage peek of what it takes to get her all put together for her magazine cover shoots. I applaud each of these women for their honesty and the courage to show up real. In a world where all too often teenagers become bulimic and middle age women starve themselves to maintain a certain image, it is essential that we all *get real* about what this is costing us on so many levels.

I have always loved beautiful clothes, and, in the early days of my career, I worked for a fashion magazine in New York City. I confess that I was *ongoingly* overwhelmed by my birds-eye view of all the fabulous models and fancy photo shoots. Being rather youthfully impressionable, it became especially easy to lose perspective in that environment and sometimes, I confess, judge myself as too fat and not beautiful "enough." It took years, and lots of personal growth books and courses, to move on to a healthier outlook.

Barbara and I met in a women's group, but our first really private encounter happened as we were standing in a ladies' room, each combing our hair. I was commenting about how mine was such a mess that day, and she confessed that she felt intimidated by me because I always seemed so fastidiously put together and confident. That honest exchange led to all sorts of confessions about our very most real feelings concerning our looks and much more. Years later, as telltale signs of aging began to appear, we made a pact that we honor to this day. It's a commitment to each other to never leave our mirrors until we can clearly see our beauty shining through, no matter what our inner emotional *chatter* is saying about what we look like at any given moment. Then we give ourselves a smile and a wink and head out into the day. It's an empowering practice that I highly recommend giving a try. Perhaps even buddy up so that you and a friend can hold each other accountable.

"You glow girl!" is a perfect affirmation worth declaring again and again to the image that greets you in the mirror each day. This is particularly true because what the years have taught me is that it is really our inner radiance that sparks our most glowing outer presence. My friend Valerie Ramsey became a first-time model rather successfully when she was in her mid-sixties, after being a stay-at-home mom to six children for most of her life. Valerie is certainly a lanky and lovely woman who exemplifies that stylish "look." Yet it is her amazing smile and glowing attitude that make her charisma on the page and on the runway so distinctive. There is a whole lot more to beauty that goes beyond formulaic preferences and some of the most startlingly unusual faces or features can be the most appealing. Consider the gap tooth smile of model Lauren Hutton, whose magnificent image graced the cover of so many magazines starting in the 1960s. Just recently I was on a website and the stunning model featured there had a harelip. Her bold and confident presence in front of the camera was so eye-catching, I immediately took notice. Every time I witness the kinds of beauty that defy convention, I am moved and inspired to both recognize each person's beautiful singularity and rest more comfortably in my own being.

When we truly open up to seeing beauty, we start to find it everywhere and in every face. Let me share the words of John O'Donohue, a favorite poet/writer of mine, to bring this idea to life. "Beyond the traffic of voyeuristic seeing, beauty waits until the patience and depth of a gaze are refined enough to engage and discover it."

It is our own patience and depth of gaze that allow us to perceive what is always available. *Have you ever noticed how those you come to know and love somehow become more and more beautiful in your eyes? Whatever your first impression might have been, it rarely stays the same as we deepen our capacity to look beyond the surface of things.*

Going back to the idea of smiling at ourselves in the mirror, one of the loveliest practices I have come across recently was in the newsletter of Michael Selzer DDS. Dentists know a thing or two about smiling, and he suggests that each night, just before going to bed, you take a full minute to invite a smile to spread across your face. Start by allowing the corners of your mouth to slowly turn upwards and then let the smile expand across your entire visage until there's a great big grin that you can feel even up to your eyes and forehead. I have been doing this for a while now and it helps ease my way into sweet dreams. Then do the same thing every morning as you wake up to greet the day. Science actually shows that the simple act of smiling programs your brain so that you feel happier. Of course, putting a smile on your face is one of the first and best ways to allow your radiance to shine through.

"There is a fountain of youth: it is your mind, your talents, the creativity you bring to your life and the lives of people you love."
~Sophia Loren, Italian film actress and singer

Every age is beautiful, and every season of our lives brings with it special gifts. These are the attributes that we come to embody with each experience we encounter along the way. As Marie Carmichael Stopes, British author and campaigner for women's rights, said, "You can take no credit for beauty at sixteen. But if you are beautiful at sixty, it will be your soul's own doing." Growing older is only a problem if you stop liking yourself as a person and no longer feel comfortable in your own skin.

There's one more lovely practice worth mentioning here. I am trained in something called the Transformation Game®, which is a board game that invites players onto a life path journey that includes insight cards, angel cards, and miracle squares along with opportunities to test their intuition and to share blessings with one another. My favorite aspect of the game occurs when a player lands on an "appreciation" square. Then each other player takes a turn telling that person what they most appreciate and admire about them. The only thing the recipient of all these favorable observations can say in return is, "Thank you. Of course. I am so glad you noticed." Isn't that delightful? How often do we deflect compliments or minimize the good things that another says to or about us? It is so difficult for us to take in and trust these positive messages. So be bold. Next time someone pays you a compliment, I invite you to respond with these exact words and see what happens.

It's Not Over Until It's Over

it's never too late
to learn to sing
or at least to move beyond
your reluctance to sing off key
to simply raise your voice
for the joy of it
or perhaps as an escape valve
for too much seriousness or sorrow

it's never too late
to make amends
or at least to find your way to peace
no matter what never was or will be
there can still be gratitude
for what quite simply is
and an opening up
to what might yet be

L ife unfolds in curious and unanticipated ways. Here I am suddenly and startlingly seventy++++…with a lot on my mind about growing (b)older. I notice that, while according to the calendar I most certainly am a certain age, within me live younger variations of myself that do not truly grasp what has happened and where the time has gone. Here I am, with all this energy and vitality and enthusiasm for life and (dare I say) a bit of wisdom gathered along the way. But we live in a society that worships youthfulness on the one hand and, on the other hand, isn't much interested in those of us who have moved beyond middle age. This prejudice is ageism: stereotyping and discrimination on the basis of age. "We're ageist any time we assume that someone is 'too old' for something—a task, a relationship, a haircut—instead of finding out who they are and what they're capable of," explains author Ashton Applewhite in her book, *This Chair Rocks: A Manifesto Against Ageism*. "Look for ways in which you are ageist instead of looking for evidence that you aren't," she urges, "because you can't challenge bias unless you're aware of it, and everyone's ageist some of the time." Applewhite goes on to make the obvious but disturbing observation that, "Ageism is a prejudice against our own future selves and takes root in denial of the fact that we're going to get old."

We know that ageism exists, all around us and within us. On the other hand, here we are, still very much alive and active and curious about what now and what next. So, while claiming to be a full-fledged grown-up or elder is not always comfortable or a particularly popular idea, what I am realizing is that these truly are golden years, a precious gift of time in which to flourish and shine.

An expression like "over the hill" always makes me wonder which hill…and then to look toward the horizon in anticipation of what next peak might be waiting for me there. Whatever life has in store over the hill or beyond the valley, count me in—or at least don't count me out! I remember first learning about the four stages of a woman's life—Maiden, Mother, Warrior, Crone (also referred to as Wise Woman)—at a retreat led by author and wise woman Joan Borysenko. I immediately embraced the idea. What is most interesting is that we don't necessarily inhabit just one stage at a time, either uniquely or sequentially. These aspects of a life fully lived overlap and we circle back through these stages again and again. There is a part of me who is still the Maiden, fertile with ideas and new opportunities to blossom. I am of course still a Mother—and a grandmother—AND a Grandmother of the larger clan/community to which I belong. I am most definitely still a Warrior Woman, offering my voice and my services to causes I believe in. And I am now stepping into and learning to embrace this Crone aspect of my life.

I made the decision to enter the relatively new profession of life and business coaching when I was in my mid-fifties. In those days the whole concept of coaching was brand new. So, when I told people that I was becoming a coach, they would ask "for what team?" I needed to elaborate in order to clarify. Since coaching can be difficult to describe (it needs to be "experienced"), I would often begin with the question, *"If you could change or create one thing in the next ninety days that would have a profound and positive impact on your life, what would that be and why?"* This inquiry created a wide variety of thoughtful answers, which led to other questions, and further responses and reflections. Then, at some point, the essential question about *how* and *when to begin* would come up—and the powerful, provocative, and action-oriented process of inquiry that is *coaching* would take hold.

Mary Catherine Bateson, author of *Composing a Life* and, more recently, *Composing a Further Life,* speaks about the ways women compose or weave their lives from seemingly disparate courses of study, jobs, careers, volunteer efforts, and lived experiences. One story that stands out in my mind is of a woman who began as an art and photography student, and then years later, after becoming a mother, decided to take a basket-weaving course with her daughter in order to spend some quality time. This mother became enamored with the beauty and technicalities of the craft and eventually traveled the world talking to and photographing weavers and their baskets. She turned those photographs and stories into a magnificent in-depth book on the subject.

As a coach I have never focused on long-term precise goals because, more often than not, when you take a step or two toward some imagined future or possibility, the Universe seems to take a step toward you, offering opportunities that didn't exist when you first started planning and taking action. No matter where you are on your life path—what decade you are entering or leaving behind—life presents new and meaningful options. The key is being ready to see them and opening your arms, mind, and heart to embrace them.

I remember being really impressed by someone who, when in her forties, began taking pre-med classes, eventually applying to and graduating from medical school and moving on to a specialty practice in radiation. When asked at her med school interviews about whether she had thought about the fact that she would be close to fifty when she completed her training, her reply was that someday she would be close to fifty in any case, so why not be doing something she is passionate about when she got there?

Another woman I know has been a hospice nurse for many years. After turning seventy, she decided that her community in Connecticut needed a small and personalized hospice facility. It took years to raise the money and do all that had to be done to turn this idea into a reality. I was with her the day she found out that the doors were about to open, and we celebrated this monumental achievement.

I have known people who left successful corporate or professional careers in their forties and fifties to start a store or launch a new business. I have known those who have launched new careers or written their first novel or painted or sculpted for the first time in their sixties and seventies. One of my most audacious female mentors, Florence Ross, went back to school for her PhD in conflict resolution at Nova University when she was in her late seventies and then went on to do work there. I have heard of elders pursuing their dreams of graduating from college and beyond even into their nineties.

A few years ago, I envisioned and then helped to organize an event at our local mall titled *New Year, New You*. Sharing the stage with me were three women. Kerry Diaz, a woman in her forties, is a wife and mother of three young children, who had left her career as a lawyer to open a clothing boutique. Diana Wilkin, a woman in her fifties left her position as the first female President of the Affiliate Relations division of CBS TV to start Twelve24 Media, a consulting firm that specializes in network relations and investment strategies. I represented the sixth decade (just under the wire at age sixty-nine), and Valerie Ramsey, fashion model, author, and motivational speaker, was our shining example of what seventy-plus could be all about. We took turns speaking about how *something* is always possible, perhaps not exactly what we had originally considered but exciting and newly challenging nonetheless.

Some of us decide to stay on our chosen career paths, honing our skills and building on our experience year after year. I know lots of coaches, psychologists, doctors, and writers who do that. There are those who have developed their creativity as a potter, a craftswoman or a painter and continue to gift the world with beautiful pieces throughout their lives. Then too there are those who retire from their careers and offer their time and considerable expertise as volunteers, rolling up their sleeves to do good work and make a difference in whatever ways they feel called to do so. And there are those, like the women who appeared with me on the stage for *New Year, New You,* who choose *rewirement*— turning their attention toward encore careers.

One of the most difficult and courageous ways that we humans reinvent ourselves is when tragedy strikes. A story that exemplifies this is close to home for me. It involves my cousins Michael and Lynn Aptman, who started the Melissa Institute www.melissainstitute.org in 1995 to honor their daughter's memory after she was killed in a carjacking incident at the age of twenty-two. As they explain, "We never felt we had any other choice in how to respond to the tragedy." The Institute promotes non-violence and supports scientific research, ensuring that the latest findings in the field are applied to reduce violence and to assist victims and their families through education, community service, support, and consultation. There are thousands of magnificent stories like these about courageous people who have endured the worst and responded in the best way possible, by building something worthwhile out of the ashes.

There is almost always *something* we can do to bring pleasure, joy, full engagement, and real meaning to our lives and the lives of others. Certainly, in terms of our character and living our values, it's always possible to ask ourselves, *"Am I the person I truly want to be at this point in my life, and, if not, what can I do to express more of my authentic self?"*

While on the subject of *it's not over till it's over* let's talk about relationships. Late life love really does happen. I have a friend whose boyfriend from more than forty years earlier showed up in her life again after she turned seventy. They eventually moved in together and, two years ago, finally married. Another friend of seventy+, twice divorced and now remarried, claims to finally be in the best relationship of her life. A third friend, who always wanted to feel "cherished" is now, in her seventies, living with a man who is making that wish come true. I have celebrated with friends and clients of all ages who have met that special someone while volunteering or going fishing or because they mustered up the courage to put their profile up on a dating website.

Life surprises us again and again with examples of just how magical and unpredictable it all can be. It also reminds us again and again of just how fragile and fleeting it all is. Isn't that reason enough to have an even greater appreciation for each and every moment that is ours to live? Most certainly, for as long as we draw breath, we all have love to give and receive and lessons to learn and share, experiences to enjoy and, when necessary, the capacity to transform our attitude in order to more than just endure the difficult ones. At the crossroads of here and now, holding this book in your hand, my hope and intention are that, page by page, you are being inspired to discover new ways to enjoy your journey and to flourish along the way. *What is calling to you now?*

Knowing Isn't Doing

show up
because it feels right
and real
because it makes
your heart sing
or sob
because it might ache
or break
if you did not
because joy lives
in the present
in your presence

just show up

If you've been around on the planet for a good number of years like I have, chances are that by now you KNOW a lot of stuff…about what *should* be important and what *should* be good for you. But, in case you forget, there are countless books and magazines and motivational speakers (myself included!) and Facebook posts to remind you. Ultimately it is up to each of us to decide which of these terrific ideas and important strategies for a lifetime are worthy of our time and effort.

Then comes the tricky part because knowing isn't doing! We need to show up for the activity (and be willing to stop the freneticism of too much activity), show up for the conversation (fully available rather than distracted), show up to take advantage of the opportunity, show up for the chance to be of service…and so much more. Every day I am learning to hold myself accountable by first deciding what would be most beneficial for me individually and then doing my best to walk my talk.

Here's something else I have noticed along the way as I have sought to strengthen my own discipline muscle and inspire my clients to do the same. Mostly, all the information and good ideas we gather along the way don't change much—but we do. We get older and savvier…or more fed up with not feeling as well as we could or not accomplishing what we say we want. So, after hearing over and over again about the same worthwhile practices that can make a difference, we finally "get it" and make the changes.

It is also important to me that those with whom I work are willing to walk their talk. For example, when I moved to Florida almost thirty years ago, it took me a long time to find a doctor who takes really good care of himself and who promotes health-wise practices before pills. It's not just about being health-conscious. I am always on the lookout for determined and dedicated coaches and other colleagues with whom to spend time…those whose conversations reflect their own commitment to focus on what's possible rather than what's not. The world is full of complainers and post-game quarterbacks, pontificating on why things went wrong or are going to hell in a handbasket. I am not interested in having my inner resources and outer wherewithal zapped by them. There is still lots of talk I want to be walking while I can.

I think that is one of the great *AHAs!* of growing through the decades. We recognize both the ticking clock and the things which most resonate with us. I heard animal rights activist Jane Goodall being interviewed at age eighty. She is a radiant being who continues to speak ardently about what matters to her, recognizing that there is still so much work she wants to do. She is hopeful that she will continue to thrive for a while longer so that she can. So do I. The world needs her presence. Indeed, I need her presence and inspiration.

Recently, I sent an email to a lovely new acquaintance, explaining why I couldn't schedule a lunch date for at least a few weeks. I took time to outline what was going on because I didn't want to seem disinterested. The *AHA! moment* for me, as I told her what I was up to—the activities that I am delighted and grateful to have the opportunity to be doing—was that I really am *mostly* walking my talk (which has most certainly not always been the case). She responded by saying, "Please tell me you are still taking time to smell the roses???"

Yes indeed. I am. It's on my list!!! For me, taking time to be present to beauty all around me is one of those essentials that needs to be more than just another good idea for which I could find a hundred good reasons to not get around to experiencing.

It's important to make it clear that this is not about anyone else feeling that they need to or, worse, *should* do what I choose to do. We each need to figure out what works for us individually to be at our best. I confess that, at this point in my life, I have learned to be particularly disciplined (not always a good thing), and I absolutely don't want it to sound overwhelming. But I have dealt with enough health challenges to know that these activities are vitally important *for me to do* in order to remain vitally well.

What is essential to note is that, as we grow older, we each ask ourselves what it is that we are preaching and teaching, what are the beliefs we hold dear and navigate by, and how are we living our values and passions to the best of our ability in this moment. The ways we choose to fill each day—all that we do and do not do, say and don't say, attend to or not, accept or not—become the way we spend our life.

Ultimately, I believe that we invite the best in others by asking the best of ourselves. *What are you asking of yourself now?*

Thirteen Ways to Move into Your Wise Woman Years

This works for the Mature Man Years as well!!!

R ev. Marsha Lehman is a coach colleague with whom I created a company called Authentic Woman Enterprises, the acronym for which was AWE. How perfect! Based on the idea of opening to, recognizing, and embracing your *AWEsomeness* here is a variation of a handout we created together. The list is thirteen ideas long because that makes for a *Baker's Dozen*—a concept that embraces giving more than expected.

1. **Find your new voice.** Time to scale new heights and hit the high notes. Discover what it is you have always wanted to speak up about and allow the perfect words and tempo and tone to bubble up from your most authentic woman-self.

2. **Flaunt your own style.** Shift from frantically following fashionable trends to displaying your own fabulous sense of flair.

3. **Attract joy.** Build your smile muscle and blast your belly laugh. Radiate happiness and become a magnet for outrageous possibilities by doing so.

4. **Become a YAY** *Sayer.* Just say YES to the gifts that life is bringing your way at this magical time of passage.

5. **Value your extra-sensitivity perception.** Rather than be upset by physical and emotional changes, embrace the ways you respond newly and freshly to everything from food to sex to spiritual awakenings.

6. **Release the energy drains** that preoccupied you in your younger more distracted days. Tap into your ripened wisdom, creativity, perspective, gratitude…these well-earned high voltage boosters.

7. **Confront your critical self.** The world is in too much trouble for you to make yourself small. You have spent precious time learning and growing into your womanly wisdom. Own it and use it.

8. **Take it all off.** Strip away the constraints that bind you and parade around in the unabashed power-full self into whom you are transforming.

9. **Dive into your fresh inklings and knowings.** Allow your mature spirit to guide and lead you as you connect with the breathtaking mysteries that surround you.

10. **Honor your values and expand your ways of living them.** Now that you have seen enough of life and have learned to remain true to your highest self, remember to continue to nurture compassion for yourself and others. Allow your perspective to be enhanced by curiosity and a growing depth of understanding.

11. **Surprise yourself.** Change can happen more swiftly and unexpectedly at this time of life. Challenge yourself to move way beyond old habits and comfort zones into undiscovered realms of amazement and delight.

12. **Leap into the grand adventure.** Allow yourself to be pulled into your clearest and highest vision of what might be possible in your home, your life, your community, and your world. In this time of transformation, you can be the change you wish to see.

13. **Flow with laughter and humor.** This is the time to NOT get stuck in a somber muck or take yourself so seriously. Revolutionize mid and later life crises into a powerful lightness of being.

Stay Curious

can you
will you
walk into this day
with the eyes of a child?

can you
will you
welcome…this moment
with a joyful heart
unencumbered
by the weight
of all you know
and all you do not know?*

Albert Einstein, the extraordinarily inquisitive physicist, admonished those he knew and mentored to "Never lose a holy curiosity." How interesting to consider curiosity "holy." Yet, without our very human penchant to be inquisitive and to wonder about the unknown, we might never have emerged from the dark ages to explore the earth, the stars or much of anything else. Perhaps curiosity, along with hope (kept from escaping from Pandora's proverbial box), are the two qualities that most inspire and direct our choices.

---

* Excerpt from a poem that first appeared in Minx Boren, *Feeling My Way—99 Poetic Journeys,* (Palm Beach Gardens, FL: Fourfold Path Inc., 2008): Page 136.

We are all in a place, whether we admit it or not, of never know-ing for sure what now or what next. Our best made plans are always vulnerable to the direction the wind is blowing and the mysteries of how whimsy has its way with us. We cling to patterns that keep us safe and yet those very same habitual behaviors can interfere with whatever *Life* may be ready to show us or shower upon us. Perhaps we believe we are staying responsibly prepared by carrying a sturdy umbrella-like mentality made of plans and strategies to protect us from the elements and elemental shifts that are bound to occur. Perhaps we choose to dis-regard the warning signs, hoping that discomfort or disaster will pass us by if we lay low or fly under the radar. Perhaps we stay oblivious, no matter the buffeting disturbances happening all around. Yet, through it all, perhaps the wise choice would be to face the music, ride the wave, surf the circumstances with easy grace and curiosity…a kind of *I-won-der-what-this-is-all-about* presence. When we can detach from our wish lists and worrisome evaluations of good/bad, better/worse, terrific/terrible and simply notice, with equanimity and grace, what is show-ing up there are unimagined treasures waiting for us to take note of and explore.

Interestingly, people who rank high on the curiosity scale are gener-ally happier. That's the finding of several studies that showed that those whose top five strengths, as measured by the VIA Signature Strengths assessment (to be found at https://www.authentichappiness.sas.upenn.edu/testcenter) include *"curiosity and interest in the world,"* actually have been found to experience benefits like a greater sense of enthusiasm and fulfillment, increased satisfaction at work and the good fortune of enjoying more meaningful experiences. Dr. Robert Biswas-Diener, positive psychologist, sited these during a talk and made the point that, given the uncertainties and increased rapidity of change nowadays, curi-osity as a positive emotional experience can be of great benefit when dealing with so many unknowns.

Can you, will you
walk into this day without
the burden of all those
preconceptions and fixed notions?
Can you, will you
open yourself to the experience
of each moment in all its peculiarities
and fascinating particulars
(even the perhaps less than pleasant ones)
even without fully grasping
the bigger picture or the grand
scheme of things?
Can you, will you somehow
let go and simply trust
that both you and the world
will benefit immeasurably
from your wide-eyed curiosity?

What if we greeted each unsubstantiated idea or inexplicable event with less fear and more easy-going interest? What if, when things don't go according to plans or preconceptions, we came from the mindset of "how fascinating" instead of "how frightening" and proceeded to explore whatever has shown up in our space or immediate worldview from that vantage point?

Not so long ago, a book I had written did not make it through test market, and my disappointment was palpable. Yet how fascinating that some of what was in that test book has now found its way into this one in a very personally satisfying version.

Bernard Baruch reminds us that, "Millions saw the apple fall, but Newton asked why." Albert Einstein humbly speaks of his own success by stating, "I have no particular talent. I am merely inquisitive." While we recognize that this is not quite true, it does make an important point because all Einstein's brilliance would have been for naught without his "holy" curiosity. These two men along with many thousands of other men and women have made our world a better place because of their inquiries into the nature of things.

Then, too, there is the curiosity within each of us about our own true nature as well as the nature of others we know or would like to know and, beyond that, about all people everywhere—and perhaps even all sentient beings. *Who am I? Who are you? What makes us tick? And why? And how?* Of course, we can never plumb the depths of what these very basic questions evoke but still how fascinating to keep asking. How rich life becomes when we dwell in all that unfolds while we simply stay curious.

Here are some basic open-ended questions that allow your genuine curiosity to invite a more in-depth conversation whenever the opportunity arises: *Would you please say more about that? How fascinating...and what else can you tell me about that? And what else? And then what happened? And then what? And then what?*

Tending the Garden
of Our Years

life reminds me again and again
of her preciousness and her fragility
the fruit set aside for tomorrow
loses its crisp freshness and rots
the moment postponed
loses its joyful spontaneity
becoming instead calculated planning...

how foolish I can be
ignoring the immediacy of life's blessings
the temporary nature of life's offerings
while all around me
flowers bloom and die

Beyond middle age we reach this precious time of harvesting and gathering—of reaping the richness of all we have planted and tended these many years. At times this requires slowing down so the fruits of our labor can mature. How do we do that? Just as marshmallows should be allowed to cook slowly over a fire until their centers have softened, just as fruit should ripen on the vine till it is full and juicy and succulent with sweetness, so too must we not try to rush the natural process of allowing our ideas to come to fruition. When tomatoes or peaches are picked prematurely and then ripened during transport, they never develop their full taste. Each thing, each possibility, each project develops at its own pace. We have only to look carefully to see what is ripening.

A life well lived includes both contemplation and exploration, both careful consideration and spontaneous exuberance, both self-containment and welcoming the words, actions, hopes, and dreams of others along our path. Wherever we have invested our time and passion, there comes a moment when we must finally stop and behold the fruits of our labors. These lessons come through loud and clear again and again. When we have devoted considerable time and passion to something, we may become impatient with wanting to push to get it done. How difficult this time of waiting can be…yet it may be *exactly* what is needed. *If there is something that you want to push or force to happen right now, might there be another way?*

So it is that questions arise as we tend to the garden of our years. *What in your life is ready to be harvested? And what might need more time on the vine?* There is a fine line between perfectly ripe and overripe or spoiled. *What is ripe in your life and work right now that might, if left too long untended, become past its prime?* For me, right now, it is this book which has been simmering and percolating for years, revealing itself one poem and one thoughtful piece of writing at a time. Here I am in the home stretch gathering and sorting and organizing and finalizing in time to take advantage of a serendipitous opportunity to get this work out into the world in a powerful way.

As we grow more fully into our later years, so many of the things to which we have devoted years to exploring and learning, creating and cultivating, reach a certain readiness. I so appreciate the arts writer Paul Gardner's remark that, "A painting is never really finished. It simply stops in interesting places." This is true of all artistic and creative endeavors. There comes a time when whatever it is that you have nurtured to fruition wants to be shared, needs to be shared, is calling out to you to be shared. Yes, of course, it can take grit and gumption and gusto and a whole lot more to actually let it out there. Do it anyway.

Today is a Good Day

today is a good day
to share
an honest smile
a piece of bread
a gentle gesture of love…

today is a good day
to be grateful
for all that is precious
and sweet and splendid
and well done

today is a good day

One of the things I love about my spin class is that, as we settle onto our bikes, the instructor always asks us to begin by "setting our intention for our ride" that day. Those simple words turn an ordinary workout into something grander and more purposeful. I am reminded that, beyond just getting through the hour-long class, I am there because I am committed to staying in shape and to having the energy, strength, flexibility, and focus to live my best life, day by day. I am also reminded of this at the beginning of each yoga session when we are asked to *dedicate our practice* to someone or something significant to us in the moment. This adds another dimension to our time on the mat by encouraging us to bring our whole Self to the postures and to remain fully present.

Perspective is everything. What we choose to pay attention to—and the ways we choose to frame our experiences—can make all the difference. On the continuum of attitudes from bad luck to a growth opportunity, from half empty to half full, from an unexpected curve ball or monkey wrench that messes with our plans to a brand new serendipitous occasion for spontaneity, from an abject failure to a learning experience—the bottom line is it's up to us.

The intentions we set for ourselves, based upon how we decide to perceive and evaluate what's showing up, influence the quality of our days and, by extension, the quality of our lives. Today is here and now, reaching out before us, ripe with delicious choices and provocative challenges, sparkling with potential and possibility—inviting us to step into it—fully alive and expansive and curious and hopeful and resilient.

Look to this day
for it is life
the very life of life…

For yesterday is but a memory
And tomorrow is only a vision.
But today well lived
makes every yesterday a memory of happiness
and every tomorrow a vision of hope.
~ANCIENT SANSKRIT POEM BY KALIDASA

Perhaps you have purchased this book for yourself because something about the concept of remembering or affirming the *AHA!* learnings of your lifetime appeals to you. Or perhaps you were gifted with this book in honor of a special occasion or because you are facing a challenging transition and someone who cares about you is seeking words to lift your spirits and awaken within you the grit and grace to carry on.

Whatever the reason, today is a gift—a once in a forever moment in time that is unfolding breath by breath. What matters and can make all the difference is that you decide beforehand that today is a blessing and an opportunity, no matter what is going on. For it is only in this moment that you can celebrate the best in life and deal with the trials, tasks, and tribulations that may present themselves.

> *"This is a wonderful day. I've never seen this one before."*
> ~Dr. Maya Angelou, American poet,
> memoirist, civil rights activist

Today is a good day to experience love, passion, creativity, meaning, accomplishment, joy, abundance, gratitude, and whatever else you choose to allow onto your radar screen and into your heart. *Is there an idea or inkling or vague sense of a possibility hovering around the periphery of your mind's eye?* Perhaps now is the perfect time to turn your attention in the direction of something you have been wanting to do or experience. There are stories of women in their later years going skydiving or learning to snorkel for the first time. There are stories of women embarking on their trip of a lifetime—checking yet another item off their bucket list.

Of course, the experience doesn't need to be spectacular to be meaningful, fun, or just plain pleasurable. Whatever is showing up in your life, today is a good day to explore it. Just like being encouraged to set an intention for my spin class, we can all be inspired to make the most of whatever is right in front of us right now and build something worthy of our time from random pieces and possibilities scattered around us. I remember taking my then almost five-year old granddaughter to a *build-a-bear* activity. There wasn't much to it really. All the bears looked exactly the same. Every child was given a bear along with a package of cotton stuffing and a tag on which to write their bear's name. But what made the experience so magical and memorable was that the very dynamic person leading the activity wove a dazzling spell of excitement and wonder. Each child was presented with a small heart that was to be tucked inside the bear. They were instructed to blow secret wishes into their bear's heart and then to kiss it three times in order to seal in all that goodness. Only then were they allowed to carefully complete the ritual by placing the red heart into the chest cavity of their new soft and furry friend. My granddaughter still has that magical bear sitting on her bed and she still reminds me that it carries her special secrets inside.

Today Is Always a Beginning

forget for a moment
how you came to be
here or why
and simply be

leave aside all
the cumbersome maps
which are after all
mere measurements that
cannot fathom or touch
the holy ground
on which you now stand...

because there is of course
no turning back
all those yesterdays
are but blessed bends
along the road to today
where now is always
a beginning*

* Minx Boren, *Healing Is a Journey: Find your own path to hope, recovery, and wellness,* (Boulder, CO: Blue Mountain Arts, 2014): Page 61.

"This is the greatest moment that you and I have ever lived. We have never been better or greater or more alive than we are right now." So says Dr. Rev. Temple Hayes, who is also a motivational speaker, the author of *Speak Unity* and *Life Rights*, and a dear friend. Over the years I have heard her make this compelling declaration again and again. Each time I am moved by the power and possibility within this statement. Temple will go on to elaborate. "As long as we believe there was a better yesterday or that tomorrow holds for us some guarantee, we are missing out on the greatest moment that you and I have ever lived and that is right now. Right now is where we have the power to change our minds, to make a decision or let go of something we no longer need, for we are truly empowered individuals."

Imagine how exciting life can continue to be at every age if we hold to the belief that the rest of our lives will add to the best of our lives. Yes, of course, circumstances change, and certain options fall away, but as long as we draw breath, we can build on all that we have already learned and experienced. We can continue to strive to be the best expression of our truest self in this very moment. It is never too late to cultivate a healthy attitude, to strengthen our character, and to take responsibility for how we show up each day and for the decisions we make. It is never too late to be kind and loving and to nurture our bodies, minds, and spiritual well-being.

As I have mentioned before, books have always been my teachers. They appear in my life just when I need to hear what they have to say. For my seventieth birthday, I was given Joan Chittister's magnificent book, *The Gift of Years*. Right from the first moment, the book spoke to me because it was filled with both wisdom and common sense. In the introduction, Chittister grabbed my attention when she referred to this time of life as "the capstone years." Webster's dictionary defines *capstone* as "the high point: crowning achievement." Chittister offers the reader an invitation to consider the added years not just a gift of more time but rather "the gift of becoming more fully alive than ever."

A friend recently sent me this quote, words by Meister Eckhart, knowing I would love it. The German theologian, philosopher, and mystic affirmed, "And suddenly you know: It's time to start something new and trust the magic of beginnings." How encouraging to trust in the mysterious possibilities inherent in initiating something new. I know women who have reinvented themselves at every age. Gayle Landen took on the presidency of the local YWCA when she was sixty-nine. Patti Burris, an artist now in her seventies, revamped her studio and is launching into a whole new series of paintings. Sandra Turnquest took on the presidency of Executive Women of the Palm Beaches after she retired from her executive position with the Florida Management District and is also launching her new career as a consultant. Dr. Amy Botwinick is a chiropractor who went through a difficult divorce, wrote a book—*Congratulations on Your Divorce: The Road to Finding Your Happily Ever After*—and has now reinvented herself as a divorce coach who helps others navigate the experience. Barbara Gay, just before turning fifty, decided to fulfill her dream of becoming a nurse. She has been working in the field for more than twenty years now. Along the way she also earned her MS and is now a senior staff member at a prestigious San Francisco hospital. Because I have been fortunate enough to have gotten to know so many extraordinary women, I could sit here all day sharing these stories of courage, ingenuity, commitment, and success.

For some who are embracing their later years, *today* is about launching into a new career or expanding a favorite hobby into a viable enterprise. For others their *carpe diem* might involve being freed up from a lifetime of responsibilities in order to finally dabble with expressing themselves in new ways and through new mediums: art, crafts, sculpting, writing, sailing, hiking, hang-gliding, mountain climbing, or photography. Then too there is traveling for the absolute joy of seeing the world or traveling with a purpose as a volunteer, learning to prepare ethnic or unusual foods for friends and family or becoming an unpaid helper in a soup kitchen or restaurant, taking up ballroom dancing or getting in shape by attending barre classes or sweating to the oldies or doing step aerobics to an endless variety of new tunes. Everything can become grist for the mill to feed our curiosity and nurture our aliveness.

The point is that, while certain possibilities may no longer be available, other opportunities appear that we could not have imagined for ourselves. An immediate example that comes to mind is that, although I love to run and was a long-distance jogger for many years, because of my two hip replacements attempting another marathon is no longer an option. Still, since I continue to love to exercise, I am now taking spin classes, doing race walking, and trying out other new types of exercise classes all the time. I am committed to showing up physically as the strongest seventy+ year old I know how to be.

> *"The best time to plant a tree was twenty years ago.*
> *The second best time is now."*
> ~Chinese Proverb

From a certain perspective, today is always a beginning. Yes, of course, yesterday has passed and tomorrow has not yet arrived. Yet, how we choose to reconsider our yesterdays—with all the blessings and lessons enfolded into even the most difficult times—and how we allow ourselves to imagine our tomorrows as opportunities to stretch and grow rather than excuses to procrastinate, are perspectives that make all the difference. These are outlooks to think about as we plan our way forward. The key is to be so fully present to the gift of the current moment that we can savor each step for its own sake. The journey *is* the destination. *The essential question becomes how can you continually find ways to enjoy yours?*

As I have said before, coaching is a process of inquiry, So, here are two other revealing questions worth reflecting upon. *What does the world need from you now? What are the specific gifts, talents, skills, and expertise that you bring to the world?* Take into consideration things like your enthusiasm, joy, optimism, and unique experiences and perceptions along with your capacity to express all these things in various ways. Perhaps another capacity that has grown with the years is your deep appreciation and gratitude for life and your ability to see beauty all around you, your discerning eye which allows you to recognize the good in others, and your good heart which encourages you to offer others your compassion and good cheer. We all need that kind of support. The world needs that kind of support. And today is most certainly a good day to offer yours.

The Gift of Three Questions

As a coach I believe in the power and inspiration of provocative and soul-searching questions. I would like to leave you with three inquiries worthy of your consideration:

1. *How do you balance your time between doing and staying active and finding quiet reflective time to contemplate the bigger "why" behind your involvements and choices?*

This book has been an invitation to dive deeply into your own inklings and learnings and knowings as you bring to light your own *AHA! moments* and to take in the *view from the perspective of your own balcony of years.* It is about discerning what matters and what counts most to you and then weighing your options based on that awareness.

2. *Are there risks you have avoided taking, for whatever reason, and what might you be willing to do now?*

As you have made your way through this book, my hope is that you have shone a light on those things that are most meaningful and significant to you. Sparked by that expanded realization, perhaps you will continue to find the gratitude, gusto, grit, grace, and a whole lot more to boldly do what is yours to do.

3. *What are the things you have done or might yet do that could qualify (by your own standards and values) as an enduring personal legacy?*

Now that you have arrived at the end of these pages, my greatest coach challenge to you is to continue on a quest to flourish and to thrive all the days of your life. Living a fulfilling life is, in its own right, an inspiration and a legacy to all those with whom you have engaged along the way. Beyond that, we simply never know about the ripple effect and the ways that our *beingness* and all that we have done during this rich journey called *life* have touched others, perhaps in myriad ways beyond our greatest imaginings.

there arrives a moment
unanticipated, unforeseen
when the magnificence of possibility
outweighs and overcomes
the risk that keeps us
holding on tight

just one step
and there it is
a bold and brave horizon
offering vast vistas
beyond our meager imaginings

and here we stand
invited to dare and trust
and perhaps leap
across the chasm of fear
or grief or presumed
inadequacy that can keep us
separated from the magnitude
of life on the other side

what will carry you across
the void?
perhaps only something as simple
as embracing your own self-worth
and your burning desire
for a life rich beyond
your wildest dreams
at every age

Addendum

A funny, fascinating, multi-serendipitous series of things happened on the way to writing, publishing, pulling off the market, and then revisiting, revisioning, revising, renaming, and, finally, republishing this book.

Because of a trademark conflict, I chose to remove the original book from Amazon. And, as I have learned, there are blessings to be found even in unforeseen and unwished for circumstances. The book you hold in your hands is better because of the drama and trauma of that incident.

Also, because of the original book, I was asked to speak at the Sage-ing International Conference in Minnesota in 2018. And, because I presented there, I met an extraordinary group of inspiring elders…and joined Elders Action Network…and took the first two of their webinar series: *The Empowered Elder* and *Choices for Sustainable Living*. I was so drawn to what in the world they are doing that I am now training to facilitate both these programs.

I was also inspired to become much more of an elder activist around issues that include the climate crisis, social justice, and environmental pollution/degradation. Most recently, I have put together and agreed to moderate a panel of experts speaking about *sustainable living* issues for a local university adult learning program. AND I have gone back to my roots as a cooking and nutrition teacher and created a program on *Food Glorious Food* that is focused on ways to nourishing both ourselves and the planet through our choices.

We seekers never know what's around the bend or what opportunities to serve might present themselves if we stay active, involved, passionate, and connected.

I urge you, dear reader, to keep your eyes, ears, mind, and heart open for your next right action. I assure you it will present itself if you stay present and willing to engage when the time is right. I wish you great and ongoing success. The world needs all our voices and our dedication… through all the decades of our lives.

With Gratitude

The actual coming together of this book is the culmination of several serendipities along with lots of ongoing support all through the process. I wonder whether anyone actually writes a book on their own. I know that I certainly haven't. First of all, within these pages there are all the stories that I am privileged to tell. Even the ones that are ostensibly about me have a cast of characters in the background who are essential to how these anecdotes, experiences, and sagas began and how they evolved. Then there are the stories that I have shared in or that have been shared with me by friends, family, colleagues, and clients. I thank each of them both for inviting me into their lives and for gifting me with narratives of their experiences. I am pleased that you, the reader, have had an opportunity to meet them throughout the book.

Then too there is this small, but significant, army of supporters cheering me on and lending their eyes, ears, expertise, endless patience, and so much more all along the journey of my getting words down on paper. An early draft of this book, at least the *bones* of it, had been put together almost two years ago. But life happens…and I broke my wrist, which required two surgeries and hundreds of hours of treatments and therapies, during which time I couldn't type much and couldn't write by hand at all.

The serendipities that jumpstarted the project again began when, at a gathering of my *tribe* of Florida coaches, the question was asked, *"What's the one thing you absolutely want to do but, for whatever reason, have been putting it off?"* When it was my turn, I mentioned this book and gave a dozen reasons why I probably should just make peace with myself and forget about it. But they weren't even vaguely interested in my reasonable excuses. "Finish the book now," they insisted. Actually, Bobbi Gemma took the time to read the early manuscript immediately and spurred me on with an extra-strong vote of confidence. So, my first big bunches of appreciative "thank yous" go to my BSS Tribe—Bobbi Gemma, Bobette Reeder, Drazia Simon, Eddie Marmol, Scott Wintrip, and Susan Klein.

Along the way, one by one, other early readers began showing up. First came Drazia, who pointed out things that really didn't belong in the book—observations that made a tremendous difference in how the book evolved. Then, because of a provocative email exchange, Lable Braun took time to thoughtfully read and comment on certain chapters. His brilliant philosophical observations were key in challenging me to make significant changes and add clarifications. Next Tova Wein, my best friend going way back to our high school days, serendipitously came for a visit. She spent half her vacation reading, commenting, cheering me on, and motivating me to focus more clearly. What a trooper! Last but not least, another friend, Ione Wiren, read the whole manuscript in three days with a really good eye and very sharp pencil. Saying "thank you" to each of these supportive angels isn't enough. When friends show up just when you need them, and do just what needs to be done, there are no words…only endless gratitude.

Writing a book can be a bit of a roller coaster process and, as I shared in the Addendum, there came a time when I had to rethink/revision/ rewrite the whole book. I became a hyper-focused woman on a mission. So huge thanks are due to my husband Mel and my family for once again *(this is not the first time I have holed up to write a book)* helping to clear the decks and making available the time and space for creativity to happen.

Another serendipitous *there-are-no-words* experience occurred just days before the original manuscript was due. I was away on retreat with my Florida tribe of coaches while trying to deal with a major revamp that needed to be done. The magic happened because their brilliant *coach approach* allowed me to see how essential it was to find my own words in certain instances where I had quoted others. They also shone a light on the whole issue of boldly using my own voice by incorporating more of my poetry, which is often where the many layers of my own thoughts are captured in a different way. Thanks are also due to Heather Hummel of PathBinder Publishing, who provided assistance with an earlier version of this book, published under a different name.

Then, in the second go-round home stretch, there was a double *OMG! serendipity* provided by Evan Griffith (*notesforcreators.com*), author of several bookitos on creativity and a terrific brainstorming partner, AND Kim Weiss, a longtime friend with a long and strong background in book marketing and publishing (*helpmewithmybook.com*). Both worked with me to come up with a new title as well as clarity about how to focus more directly on a *coach approach* that would provide greater benefit to readers.

And then a third serendipity occurred as I was contemplating republishing. My dear and longtime friend Betz Rothstein generously offered me additional support in ways I had not even considered. What I find so interesting about all these fortunate occurrences is that they confirm my belief that, when something is meant to happen and the timing is right, all kinds of magical and meaningful circumstances and "forces" (and a bunch of really great friends) conspire to move things forward.

Great appreciation is due to Carol and Gary Rosenberg—The Book Couple—who took on the project of getting the re-visioned, reworked, and retitled manuscript into book form and out into the world. It was such a delight working with this dynamic duo. First of all, they are really good listeners and took the time to get a handle on my concerns and what I wanted to achieve. And they are amazingly creative and enthusiastic, which made the whole process *stress-less* and fun.

Finally, an *extra special worth repeating* thank you to my husband Mel and my son Reid for listening…and listening…and listening some more…and then providing ideas and support that made all the difference. Honestly, without the two of you, I do not know how it all would have turned out.

About the Author

Minx Boren MCC is a master certified coach, credentialed through the International Coach Federation. Coach Minx is also a writer, poet, columnist, motivational speaker, workshop facilitator and adjunct professor at FAU—Osher Lifelong Learning Institute. She is the author of four books of poetry, co-author of eight books for women, and author of two *life journey* books: *Healing Is a Journey—find your own path to hope, recovery, and wellness* and *Friendship Is a Journey—a celebration of true connection and deep caring.*

For almost thirty-five years, Minx has been developing and presenting innovative programs that support health and balance, creativity and effectiveness, and reflection and achievement. As a life coach, her focus is on not only what it means to live a joyful, meaningful, and fulfilling life but also what it takes to do so. Minx partners with others, individually and in groups, who are seeking ways to express their best selves and live their best lives. Because of her chosen vocation and calling, Minx is always inquiring into what gives LIFE to life–what awakens our creativity and passion, our dreams and resourcefulness, and our will and willingness to do the next right thing. Her ongoing quest is to shine a light on all that allows us to flourish and to be our most radiant selves.

Minx is active in her community and has served as President of Executive Women of the Palm Beaches 2013/2014 and as a Board Member of the Women's Foundation of Palm Beach County since 2007. She is a 2013 recipient of the Giraffe Award, presented by the Women's Chamber of Commerce to women who "stick their necks out for others." Coach Minx is a member of the National Association of Professional Women (NAPW) and has been awarded the status of Pinnacle Professional by Continental Who's Who.

Most recently, Minx has become involved in Elders Action Network and is currently co-facilitating webinars on *The Empowered Elder* and *Sustainable Living* and serving on their Leadership Council as well as contributing to their newsletter. To find out more, visit Elders Action.org.

To find out more about Minx's work,
visit her website CoachMinx.com.